Two and Two

Pitt Poetry Series

Ed Ochester, Editor

DENISE DUHAMEL

Two and Two

UNIVERSITY

OF PITTSBURGH

PRESS

The publication of this book is supported by a grant
from the Pennsylvania Council on the Arts

Published by the University of Pittsburgh Press,
Pittsburgh, PA 15260

They, and every beast after his kind, and all the cattle after their kind, and every creeping thing that creepeth upon the earth after his kind, and every fowl after his kind, every bird of every sort.

And they went in unto Noah into the ark, two and two of all flesh, wherein is the breath of life.

Genesis 7:14–15

CONTENTS

Two and Two

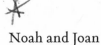

Noah and Joan

It's not that I'm proud of the fact
that 20 percent of Americans believe
that Noah (of Noah's Ark) was married
to Joan of Arc. It's true. I'll admit it—
Americans are pretty dumb and forgetful
when it comes to history. And they're notorious
for interpreting the Bible to suit themselves.
You don't have to tell me we can't spell anymore—
Ark or Arc, it's all the same to us.

But think about it, just a second, timeline aside,
it's not such an awful mistake. The real Noah's missus
was never even given a name. She was sort of milquetoasty,
a shadowy figure lugging sacks of oats up a plank.
I mean, Joan could have helped Noah *build* that ark
in her sensible slacks and hiking boots. She was good with swords
and, presumably, power tools. I think Noah and Joan
might have been a good match, visionaries
once mistaken for flood-obsessed and heretic.

Never mind France wasn't France yet—
all the continents probably blended together,
one big mush. Those Bible days would have been
good for Joan, those early times when premonitions
were common, when animals popped up
out of nowhere, when people were getting cured
left and right. Instead of battles and prisons
and iron cages, Joan could have cruised
the Mediterranean, wherever the floodwaters took that ark.

1

And Noah would have felt more like Dr. Doolittle,
a supportive Joan saying, "Let's not waste any time!
Hand over those boat blueprints, honey!"
All that sawing and hammering would have helped
calm her nightmares of mean kings and crowns,
a nasty futuristic place called England.
She'd convince Noah to become vegetarian.
She'd live to be much older than nineteen, those parakeets
and antelope leaping about her like children.

Egg Rolls

I was walking down First Avenue and knew
my check wouldn't clear for another two days and I had two tokens
and a can of tuna at home and an old roll which wouldn't be so bad
if I warmed it up in the oven and there was some cheese they let me take home
from the graduate student reading except my roommate had already eaten
most of it   he was pretty good about not touching my stuff but I guess he knew
this wasn't really "mine" in the sense that I hadn't paid for it
since it was just rolled up in some party napkins   half of it sliced
the other half a big cube and I had exactly seven dollars in my pocket
which was my train fare to and from school the next day
I went to Sarah Lawrence where the flowers were in bloom
and everyone in the town had shiny blond hair and pastel turtlenecks
and I tutored a woman who had all her meals catered   macrobiotic
delivered right to her dorm and I knew she'd feel bad for me if she knew
I ate fish from a can   she'd feel bad like my dad did the time he visited me
and he saw my thirty-nine-cent chili that I bought from a supermarket cart
where they dump all the food with expired codes and the dented cans
and my father said don't eat this   you could die   of botulism
and I felt like I'd botched up and that botulism was a disease
that hit people like me who didn't have enough to open a checking account
who cashed checks and just lived off the money until it was gone

it's easy to feel sorry for my former self
the one that wanted to go to grad school so bad she was a nanny
and a receptionist and taught at a nursery school and cashed all her savings bonds
to buy a two-hundred-dollar-car that died the day after she bought it
because she hoped it would make her life easier and the mechanic said
it would take at least nine hundred dollars to fix so she just junked it and refused to eat
because everything she tried was an ugly mistake a sour bargain
and there was no way she could get ahead or even make the time to feel her angst

to write a good workshop poem since she had to be at her job at five
in the morning where she was a receptionist in a health club
and they gave her a big gold key that looked like a key to the city
and she was the first one to get there and turn on the whirlpool
and sort the accounts and vacuum the carpet where rich women did aerobics
and she only worked until one so it seemed like a good job and her boss told her all
about the new diets   that if you just waited until dinner to eat
then you could eat a whole pot of rice and that was only something like 600 calories
and stay away from cherries and grapes and all small fruits because the smaller
the fruit the more sugar and she was supposed to eat apples because that's how
you get the most fiber with the least amount of calories and calories
that's what everyone talked about and she was so tired and hungry
that by the time she arrived at Sarah Lawrence she fell asleep in her literature class
and she knew it was an insult to the professor who was stern and took it seriously

and she did too so that's when she learned about coffee and diet pills
and how to stay awake even on days when she woke up at 3:30 a.m. and took a shower
in the dark since the shower was in the kitchen where her roommate slept
and she didn't want to wake him up even though she must have woken him
the water itself hissing in that plastic stall and she usually tripped on something and she
had begun to hate him anyway since she found his rent bill and he was charging her
$450 even though his rent was only $500 and that was just New York her friends said
she shouldn't confront him he could kick her out and where else
was she going to live for $450 a month   just ignore the mother cockroach she saw
diving in the bread crumbs and the baby cockroaches that scattered
in the kitchen sink and the hot pipe she burned her leg on every time she peed
because that toilet was so small and the soles of her feet were black with grime
because she couldn't get the floor clean and why should she try
she was paying most of the rent   she shouldn't have to be the maid too
her bedroom was so small she had to roll her futon up if she wanted anyplace to stand
and she wrote her poems with her typewriter on her lap but still she wrote them and
she never felt so bad for herself really because she was in New York

on the corner of First Avenue and First Street where everything began
and most of the time she felt like she had everything
except that time she smelled those egg rolls
the ones wafting from the Chinese restaurant and she told herself

maybe I should run home and sell my subway tokens to my roommate and walk
the forty blocks to work tomorrow in the frigid dark and have one of those egg rolls
the ones with shrimp bits and light green vegetables inside and I fingered
my seven dollars   the five and two ones I carried with me
just in case the apartment was robbed and I stopped and looked in the window
the egg rolls lined up like sleeping bags under fluorescent light and the cook smiled
the Chinese man with a gray ponytail and white bibbed apron and I went in
and asked how much and bought two because they were small
and ate them on the street   grease burning my lower lip
the hot insides burning the roof of my mouth   you're supposed to drink milk
that's the only way to cure that scorch   something about the protein
healing the cells of the tongue but I had no milk so I blew into the egg roll
like a mother blowing on her baby's spoon
or like a diva testing a microphone and the whole city hushed
as I squeezed the greasy napkin and it was like I was singing a torch song
but I wasn't that sad that I wouldn't have the money to go to school tomorrow
or that my diet was shot and I actually remember feeling kind of rich

Crater Face

is what we called her. The story was
that her father had thrown Drano at her,
which was probably true, given the way she slouched
through fifth grade, afraid of the world, recess
especially. She had acne scars
before she had acne—pocks and dips
and bright red patches.
                    I don't remember
any report in the papers. I don't remember
my father telling me her father had gone to jail.
I never looked close to see the particulars
of Crater Face's scars. She was a blur, a cartoon
melting. Then, when she healed—her face,
a million pebbles set in cement.
                    Even Comet Boy,
who got his name by being so abrasive,
who made fun of everyone, didn't make fun
of her. She walked over the bridge
with the one other white girl who lived
in her neighborhood. Smoke curled
like Slinkies from the factory stacks
above them.
                    I liked to imagine that Crater Face
went straight home, like I did, to watch Shirley Temple
on channel 56. I liked to imagine that she slipped
into the screen, bumping Shirley with her hip
so that the child actress slid out of frame, into the tubes
and wires that made the TV sputter when I turned it on.
Sometimes when I watched, I'd see Crater Face
tap-dancing with tall black men whose eyes

looked shiny, like the whites of hard-boiled eggs.
I'd try to imagine that her block was full
of friendly folk, with a lighthouse or goats
running in the street.

       It was my way of praying,
my way of un-imagining the Drano pellets
that must have smacked against her
like a round of mini-bullets,
her whole face as vulnerable as a tongue
wrapped in sizzling pizza cheese.
How she'd come home with homework,
the weight of her books bending her into a wilting plant.
How her father called her slut, bitch, big baby, slob.
The hospital where she was forced to say it was an accident.
Her face palpable as something glowing in a Petri dish.
The bandages over her eyes.

       In black and white,
with all that makeup, Crater Face almost looked pretty
sure her MGM father was coming back soon from the war,
seeing whole zoos in her thin orphanage soup.
She looked happiest when she was filmed
from the back, sprinting into the future,
fading into tiny gray dots on UHF.

7

The Problem with Woody Allen

(even before Soon Yi)
is that he breaks up with people
like Mariel Hemingway (in *Manhattan*)
and Diane Keaton (in *Annie Hall*)
without so much as a joke about his scrawny body,
those parody glasses, his sallow skin.
My friend Rhonda said (about *Deconstructing Harry*),
"Elisabeth Shue should get an Oscar
for making out with Woody Allen
and not throwing up!" At least
Elisabeth gets to dump him, but still—
why does Woody Allen's character cheat
on Judy Davis? I see what he was trying to do
in *Celebrity,* projecting his male fantasies
through Kenneth Branagh, who's a little easier
to look at. But would Melanie Griffith really give
Kenneth Branagh/Woody Allen a blow job?
I understand if she wants to get a part in the movie
Celebrity, but she's already in it, playing a famous actress,
and Kenneth Branagh is supposed to be
a lowly journalist, so, frankly, it doesn't make sense.
Even Winona Ryder, playing a struggling actress,
falling for Branagh is a stretch.
Wasn't she just going out with Matt Damon
in real life?
      So when I stumble upon
Allen's latest film treatment—he's starring in his films again,
he just can't help it—I feel compelled to write to him
about my concerns:

Dear Mr. Allen, I'm afraid
this time you're really going to embarrass yourself.
A nursing home patient (you) getting sexual gratification
from a student nurse (Gwyneth Paltrow)? I admit
the premise sounds fun, even madcap—Gwyneth
loves you so much that when you beg her
she sneaks you out of Palm Springs's Golden Gables
and takes you cross-country, popping open your cans
of Ensure and playing her "young people" music
while you kvetch and cover your ears.
The fish-out-of-water element is intriguing—
you hyperventilating as Gwyneth forces you to peer
over the Grand Canyon. You reading the ingredients
of Gwyneth's Pepsi One can with a magnifying glass.
But would you really leave Gwyneth
when you meet up with neurotic Drew Barrymore,
a displaced New Yorker teaching philosophy
in North Dakota? Would Drew really be visiting
the Lawrence Welk Museum when you walk in
(because Gwyneth drops you off there
so she can go mall shopping in peace)?
Would Drew really let you move in
immediately, after that first kiss
behind Welk's favorite accordion? Would you really
leave your oxygen tank behind in Gwyneth's trunk?
Would Gwyneth in a rage really flush all your prescriptions?
Would Drew risk everything for you, even her tenure?
Would you (as a runaway nursing home patient) really
be able to balance on the back of Drew's Harley
all the way from Grand Forks to the Upper East Side?

Incest Taboo

It always freaked Jane out when her father
called her mother "Mommy," as in "Mommy,
let's pack up the car and go for a drive!"
Jane grew up to be afraid of birds.
She swerves now whenever a sparrow swoops
toward her windshield. She can't go to the beach
because of the seagulls that dive and circle
like hornets or warplanes. Even humming-
birds creep her out, the way they just hover
quivering like they are about to explode.
Blue jays, robins, even doves have wronged
her, one way or the other. All lousy parrots.

Jane was changing her bathing suit at the beach
house her parents rented. It was a parrot-
green one-piece with a yellow swoop
of daisies down the front. It was wrong
the way her brother Fred barged in—the bird
brain—without knocking, his voice exploding,
"Hurry up! The drive-in
starts in two minutes!" He hovered,
her suit rolled down around her hips. "Mommy
wants to leave now," he said, leering. The hum
of a car engine out front, their father
honking. Then Fred backed away. Jane's suit left wet circles

on the floor. On the movie screen, explosive
wings and Tippi Hedren. Two clean semicircles
arched the dusty windshield, a splatter of white bird
poop the wipers couldn't reach. Their father

yelled, "Mommy! Look at that! They're running the wrong
way!" Seawater sloshed in Jane's ears, humming,
the soundtrack fading in and out, dialogue swooping
from the crackling gray box hanging from her mother's
window. Fred avoided looking at her. He parroted
bird screeches. His fat greasy hands hovering
over the popcorn made Jane say, "You ugly beached
whale! Share! . . . Mom and Dad, look, Fred's driving

me to drink!" "That's enough," their father replied, hum-
drum dad-talk, as though the drive-in
was as good a place as any to announce her wrong
turn, to foreshadow her own alcoholism. Beach
bunny Jane, fourteen, with a father
as good or bad as most, a hovering
mother. Did she know then she'd wind up terrified of birds—
hunched under barstools, screaming about the parrot
on Baretta's shoulder? The next day Jane circled
the beach house block on a rusty bike. "My mother's
a bitch," she said, meaning Fred. Freckles exploded
on her arms. Her ponytail, a bright chestnut swoop.

Years later, at the party, Jane's husband hovers
over her, trying to control her drinking, swooping
toward each rum and coke, like a father
trying to save the boiler before it explodes,
like a mother bargaining with the beach—
"Give me back my son and I'll be the best mother
in the whole world! I know I was wrong
to let Fred swim alone." She'd trusted that circle
the sun made in the sky, but never again. "Jane drives
herself crazy with regret," her husband says, a parrot

to her whims. The party is humming
with rumors, guests screeching like dawn-inspired birds.

Jane never wanted to become a mommy.
That is, she wanted to stay sexy, unburdened
by diapers. She wanted to walk a birdless beach
without a string of toddlers behind her, pull-toys humming.
She was sure her body would explode
during childbirth. She dreamt of parrots,
instead of babies, flying through her legs. Her father
had wanted a boy, someone he could teach to drive
golf balls into the future, someone he could swoop
down and lift to the basketball hoop, a circle
of victory. He had Fred who hovered
behind him, a cub, until everything went wrong.

Jane says the same words over and over, a parrot
who wants her Prozac-cracker. Her therapist wears the wrong
colors—spring, though she's clearly an autumn. Explosive
dinosaur earrings brush her neck, hover
near her collar. Jane's distracted, humming
"The Wind Beneath My Wings," drawing a circle
around each question. "If we'd rented a beach
house, I think I'd remember!" Jane's father's voice swoops.
He reminds Jane that Fred was a good son, a boy scout. *The Birds*
is her least favorite movie. "What drive-in?
We never went to any drive-ins," Jane's mother
insists. "I don't like mosquitoes. Just ask your father."

How can Jane break the incest taboo circling
her own marriage? Her husband looks less like her father
when he wears her lingerie. Jane doesn't hum

even when he's sick—she won't soothe him like a mommy.
Every girl is part Jane, hovering
around puberty, a sleazy corner. Adults drive
by quickly so they won't remember their imploding
hearts, nothing ever as intense again. Bird-
watching aggravates Jane. "It's wrong,"
her mother said, talking about *girl* watching, Fred's swooping
eyes scanning breasts and thighs, his mouth parroting
his friends' dirty talk. All winter he waited for the beach.

Baretta's parrot, also named Fred, drives
Jane to think about that moldy beach
house where Fred picked up her wet suit. His voice hovered
close to her ears. "Everything's related. Parrots
descend from dinosaurs. That's why mommy
is afraid of them," Fred said, swooping
Jane's bathing suit into the air, humming
a Donny and Marie love song. "You're *so* wrong!"
Jane said, about the parrots with dinosaur grandfathers.
Fred locked her door with a hook that looked like a bird's
beak and flapped his arms like seagull wings, circling
a fish who was Jane. Her insides exploded

as he pushed her on the twin bed, his palm swooping
over her mouth. Now the radio explodes
I'm a bitch. I'm a lover. I'm a child. I'm a mother . . .
trying to shock her with its top ten song, circle
lyrics that make Jane wish she still had that parrot-
green bathing suit that proved her bird-
bee-beeing brother walked in on her, then hovered.
That proved he came in again, after her father
left to take a midnight walk on the beach

all by himself. Jane didn't think her father was wrong
to take the car out alone and just drive—
to want out as her mother stayed in the shower, humming.

Fred liked to shoot things, especially birds,
which were more challenging than cans. His guns hummed
with promises of taxidermy. Parrot-
sized birds he couldn't name were driven
out of trees and plopped dead in circles
onto the ground. Jane knew killing was wrong,
even birds, and she'd yell to her mother,
"Make him stop!" She waited for beach
weather, then buried her son's fun, explosive
pangs of anger in her chest. "You're his father,
talk to him," she said as her husband swooped
his fork to his plate—Jane crying, silence hovering.

Jane finally felt happy, though she knew it was wrong.
At Fred's funeral, his girl-watching buddies hovered
near the casket, crying in huddles, circles
football players make before they swoop
and clobber the other team. Jane was learning to drive.
She'd missed driver's ed to stand with her father
near the casket. Jane's mother kept fainting, parroting,
"Thanks for coming," to the mourners whose grief exploded
like shaken soda bottles. Sometimes she still hears them hum
like she did that summer at the beach
when bottles popped right on 7-11 shelves. A bird-
like cashier. Glass shards. Her father yelling, "Look, mommy!"

Look at that!" Jane's father and mother
still don't remember seeing Hitchcock's *The Birds*

or the swooping seagulls. Even the beach house
is caught in a blurry circle of memory, humming
and hovering, ready to explode. It doesn't help
Jane gets details wrong—Baretta had a cockatoo, not a parrot.

Napping on the Afternoon of My Thirty-ninth Birthday

A man sits between my husband and me at the movies, then puts his hand on my breast and says, "Let's go." I say, "Excuse me, I'm here with my husband . . ." But my husband hushes me and points to the screen. The man says, "Your wife and I will meet you in the lobby," and without looking up, my husband says, "OK." The man pushes me against the wall—he has some kind of coarse beard and his pubic hair is all prickly. I'm screaming for my husband, but he never comes. I don't do anything to save myself—no karate chop, no biting, no clawing. I want to be saved by my husband, but I'm not.

The bearded man takes me to a rodeo and says, "This is how it's done." The big animals are fucking and the females are screaming—they aren't bulls or cows, but something even fiercer. I say to the man, "You are my nightmare." Then the same man is buying me ice cream and we are friends, maybe even married. My real husband never comes to get me, which probably has nothing to do with him, but instead is about my anxiety. It may even be a basic lesson—how I have to save myself. Or a primitive fantasy that I want to be taken, no matter how brutal. Most probably, it's all about fear.

In the hall I meet up two women who have been scorned, and we storm into the man's apartment. I'm going to help them do what—kill him? We are dressed like Charlie's Angels and the man is the same man who raped me, who then bought me ice cream. He is watching some kind of pornography—women and snakes. We toss the TV on top of him. His feet curl up, a la the Wicked Witch, while the TV smokes and our clothes evaporate. Then we are, all three of us, women with big round butts and tiny waists. We prance around wearing only gossamer wings, the height of desire on a nineteenth-century sepia postcard.

Dream Interpretations

Each woman with wings is Lady Luck 13, and the three of you equal thirty-nine (your age).

You were an angel then, and you're an angel now.

"Coarse" meaning "intercoarse," a coarse, unpleasant penetration.

This is all a fantasy, as the set-up scene is in a movie. In a dream, you basically star in your own movies.

You want to embarrass yourself by telling this dream. You want to take confessional poetry to its ultimately foolish heights.

You are a lesbian.

You want a three-way.

You are full of rage, and the TV has to pay.

An aspect of your personality is expressed by each of the people in your dream—you are, in addition to the "I," also the inattentive husband, the rapist, the brutal male animals, the female animals being hurt, and a woman longing for a safe way to express sexuality.

You should take martial arts lessons as well as some sort of flying lessons (plane or windsurfing perhaps).

You feel like your husband doesn't notice you enough. Try a new perfume?

You are anxious about getting older and your body changing in a youth culture such as ours. (You romanticize the nineteenth century, thinking that perhaps it was better for older women then. Also your body type was more popular and desirable then.)

You are afraid you will grow your own beard as your hormones begin to change.

Three women. The trinity? Are you Christian?

If you, the reader, have any other keys to unlocking this dream, please send them, in the form of a poem or prose poem, to the publisher of this volume.

Our Americano

An apple-pie Americano—attaboy!—got the ax for being asleep at the switch and
back-talking his backasswords ball-busting boss. Though our Americano was a bit of
  a blowhard, he wasn't a bad egg. His being bagged by his boss made him feel like
  he had belly-flopped in his birthday suit. Basically, he was over a barrel, with the
  bejesus knocked out of him, and no matter how hard he beat his brains out, he
  remained betwixt and between. What if he was a bozo bullshit artist who couldn't
  see the big picture? Maybe, he thought, he should bootlick, belly up to his big shot
  of a boss. He sat in the
can thinking about being canned. He decided he was no comma-counter, no company
  man. He chugalugged a beer and chowed down Chinese. His chips being so down
  led him to the cathouse where he carried a torch for a cat's-meow call girl named
  Nicole who could do one crazy cement mixer. Though he wasn't her cup of tea,
  the cutie pie didn't give him the cold shoulder. Instead, she cased out his
dick and poured him a double, which made him feel less like a dead duck. After his
  night out, he was dead broke, a desperado divvying up his double-decker sand-
  wich. He had one last chance—his hot-diggity demo he took to a doozy of a deejay
  in a dinky a.m. station. The deejay said, "You're no dreamboat, but you sound
  damn fine." Our Americano knew these were his dog days, but he was an
eager beaver on the eighty-eight. He hoped elbow grease and an Elvis haircut could
  get him to Easy Street, but meanwhile he moved into a
flea-trap flophouse full of fancy pants and floozies. He took forty winks and dreamed
  of being the filthy rich, fashion-plate, fair-haired boy who finagled a fast buck
  with his forty-five. His fans were finger poppers who flipped their lids whenever
  they heard his name. He liked living in a fishbowl where he could futz around in a
  five-and-dime and—
gee whiz!—googols of gussied-up glamour girls would go gaga. He'd take a gander at
  their great gams, then make goo-goo eyes—each one would have Nicole's face,
  giving him the go-ahead. He was on a gravy train, his groovy gold-star gimmick a
  gas. Then the gall! His god-awful alarm clock and the realization his dream was a

gag gift. He was back to being a greenhorn again, a goose egg, a goof-off, a goon. He was back to the grind, a

hayseed, a half-assed horse's ass, a hack. A hammy ham-and-egger in hand-me-downs who'd had it, who'd have to pass the hat in hopes that highfalutin hoity-toity higher-ups who lived high on the hog would have a heart and give him a hand-out. He needed a headshrinker for his hang ups, a headhunter who was also a hot sketch. If only he could get a job as a hubba-hubba heartthrob. His hell-hole apartment was giving him the heebie-jeebies. Just when he was thinking that maybe he should

ixnay the ivory thumper dream and iron out things with his icky former boss, the deejay called to say that our Americano was in like Flynn, the he was the new "it boy." He hit the

jackpot. Jailbait Janes and Joe Colleges alike were jazzed up over the jingle-jangle of his forty-five. He owed it all to the deejay, the jim-dandy who saw the jism in his jitterbug. No longer Joe Blow, no longer John Doe, our Americano jumped off the deep end and put his John Hancock on a contract agreeing to jazzy jam sessions and keeping up with the Joneses. He traded in his jalopy for a Jaguar with a jazzy radio and jiffy power steering—the whole

kit and caboodle. He was suddenly kingpin. Kids from Kentucky to Kazoo were keen for his new

LP, the one where he lollygagged like a loverboy on the cover, a long drink of water turned into a lone-wolf ladies' man by his agent. Loudmouth lounge lizards, lovebirds, letches, and lowlifes on the lam all learned the lingo of our livewire loco Americano.

Madison Avenue masterminded a memo to make sure he was *the* make-out artist on Main Street, the man-about-town on every main drag, the Real McCoy, Mister Right. Even his meshuggeneh mumsy was mad about his moxie. Martooni in hand, our Americano wanted to mooch, to make it with his main squeeze before he was slipped a Mickey Finn, before the mudslinging that went along with the monkey business of stardom began. He went back to the

notch-house he went to as a nobody from noplaceville, took a number, waiting along with the other nudniks, and asked for Nicole. Nope, they said, no dice. No-good

Nicole was nixed for taking a nosedive, for using needle candy. The nervy madam said, "What about Nina? Nancy? Noel?" "No!" said our heartbroken Americano. "Don't knock it," said the madam, "don't be so nitpicky," using her noggin, thinking about her nest egg. But only Nicole was our Americano's

oomph girl, his one and only, the only one he could open up to, the only one on his one-track mind. He searched for her in oodles of offbeat streets. It was like someone had given him a one-two punch when he heard she'd ODed. He drank one too many on-the-house drinks. Fans gave him the once-over, but he was out to lunch. His friend the deejay gave him a

pep talk then, as a picker-upper, took him to a peep show where pinup girls in plunging necklines polished off Dom Perignon. He was a party pooper besieged by posh party girls who tried to get palsy-walsy, but our Americano pleaded the fifth. Even though his next pop song was panned, his agent, a phonus bolonus, assured him he was popular in passion pits everywhere, the prez of the post-Elvis look, page-one news. Our Americano now dreamed of his pencil-pushing days, dreams in which his pink slip never came and he was

quick on the uptake, giving every job the quick-over, stopping for a quick one at the bar on his way home to a

run-of-the-mill rundown ranch house where Nicole would be roasting a roast. He missed the rat race, the rinky-dink rubber checks, rubbing elbows with the rowdy and raunchy. His mother pulled rank and told him he had rocks in his head, that he just needed a little R and R, and a red-hot mamma to help him to stop rehashing Nicole. He needed razzle-dazzle razzmatazz, the red carpet.

"Stop being such a sad sack," she said. "Your setbacks are small potatoes, smidgen-sized snafus. Savor your salad days, your saddle shoes, your sass and savvy say-so, your Shangri La where you shake a wicked calf. You go stag to shindigs and shimmy with sexpots. You've earned your sheepskin in slap-happy sashaying and super-duper stargazing. And don't forget your standout smash hit that gives the girls the screaming meemies! I know I'm no spring chicken, but I'm not from Squaresville either. I know the scoop, and I know the score. Don't be a screwup! Don't be a sap! I'm not going to sugarcoat it, son, you're a swellelegant somebody,

the only chance I have left for a sugar daddy!" And with that, she skedaddled
from the soap opera of our Americano's life. He
took five to take it all in, his tearjerker of a life in 3-D. His mother's two cents' worth
of a tailor-made third degree was just the ticket that made him realize he was
being a tightwad with his talent. He went to Tin Pan Alley where he wrote tip-
top, topnotch torch songs for Nicole, his departed tart.
Umpteen undergrads—uppity, cool and uncool alike—threw undies and other
unmentionables as our Americano sang, a real
Valentino, a VIP who made vamps of
wallflowers with his wails and wiggle. He gave his weepies their walking papers, and
soon he was the water-cooler talk of wisenheimers and windbags. Women wolf-
whistled at him. He made whoopee with one wiry wham-bam-thank-you-
ma'am who became his wonderful wife. He had the wherewithal, wads of what it
takes, the
x-factor. In fact, his x marked the spot. Our Americano was an example to
yackety-yak yes-men everywhere. He inspired a
zillion Zen hipsters, zoot-suiters, and zazoos with his zing, zazzle, and zowie.

Pituitary Theft

GOOD GUY:

I am damn unsatisfied to be killed in this way, I can tell you that much. I would much prefer a painless coronary or even cancer so I'd have a chance to say goodbye to my friends. Instead, you twirl that gun like a baton. My stomach throbs from where your thugs continue to kick.

BAD GUY:

Damn, I'll burn you into a BBQ chicken if you don't stop your whining. Are you not my strong foe? Fight back, you young kitten, you vulva and vagina.

GOOD GUY:

You always use violence. I should've ordered glutinous rice chicken then you would have seen *real* violence as I chewed with my mouth open and stuck out my food-laden tongue! I am a real man. Do you think I really care about a chicken's life?

BAD GUY:

Quiet or I'll blow your throat up!

GOOD GUY:

You are sick, I hope you know that. A normal person wouldn't steal pituitaries.

BAD GUY (to THUGS):

Beat him out of recognizable shape! (Then to GOOD GUY) Beware! Your bones are going to be disconnected!

GOOD GUY:

Ha! You think those glands will really make you rich? Only *I* know where they keep the hypothalamus and thyroid. (to THUG ONE) Fatty, you with your thick face have hurt my instep! Ouch!

BAD GUY:

Thug, stop. (To GOOD GUY) What did you say?

GOOD GUY:

I said I know where they keep the hypothalamus and—

Suddenly, SPIDER WOMAN swings into the damp chamber.

BAD GUY:

Yah-hah, evil Spider Woman! I have captured you by the short rabbits and can now deliver you violently to your gynecologist for a thorough extermination.

SPIDER WOMAN:

Not so fast, bad guy! Perhaps this is who you are looking for. Do you recognize this dead gynecologist who I carry over my shoulder as easily as a sack of wheat?

BAD GUY AND THUGS:

Your rancid web has smothered another. But why Ralph? He was just an OB doing his job!

GOOD GUY:

Spider Woman, don't let them make you feel guilty! They've stolen the pituitaries!

SPIDER WOMAN (whipping out her Uzi):

Just as I suspected.

BAD GUY:

I got knife scars more than the number of your leg's hair!

THUG ONE:

Oh no! Gun wounds again?

24

SPIDER WOMAN:

Shut up, all of you! I am sure you will not mind that I remove your manhoods and leave them out on the dessert flour for your aunts to eat.

THUGS:

Please no! Anything but our manhoods!

BAD GUY (to SPIDER WOMAN):

Perhaps we can *split* the pituitaries, my pretty one? Surely, even Spider Woman can be tempted by the thought of making a little gland money on the side?

SPIDER WOMAN:

Do not dare to bribe me with your stolen body parts! Take my advice, or I'll spank you without pants!

BAD GUY:

I have been scared shitless too much lately.

GOOD GUY:

Spider Woman, you look lovely today. Would you be so kind as to pull this knife from my arm? One of the thugs has left it in me to fester.

SPIDER WOMAN:

Yes, my friend. And thank you for noticing my feminine charms. I live in fear that people will recognize that I am really a man, what with my big muscle arm and abundance of facial hair.

GOOD GUY:

Nonsense, Spider Woman. You are a beautiful large black person. Let us not forget to form a team up together and go into the country to inflict the pain of our karate feets on some ass of the giant lizard person.

SPIDER WOMAN:

Yes, we can be sure that giant lizard person is at the bottom of all this pituitary theft!

GOOD GUY:

But first, let us torture and kill the bad guy and his thugs for they have shown meanness.

SPIDER WOMAN shoots BAD GUY and THUGS.

BAD GUY:

The bullets inside are very hot. Why do I feel so cold?

THUG ONE:

How can you use my intestines as a gift?

SPIDER WOMAN (hurling the GYNECOLOGIST toward THUG ONE): Die near this already-dead vagina-peering man!

GOOD GUY:

Hurry, Spider Woman. We have no time to waste. There is the anatomy of all Hong Kong to save!

Warning

Do not swallow.

If you accidentally swallow this poem, contact a poison control center immediately.

Do not read this poem while sleeping.

If you consume three or more alcoholic drinks every day, consult your doctor before reading this poem as a pain reliever.

This poem is not for use with the browning unit of your conventional oven.

Never place this poem in a microwave.

This poem may cause stomach bleeding.

In case of bleeding, consult a doctor promptly.

Do not take this poem by mouth or place in nostrils.

Do not put this poem into the rectum by using fingers or any mechanical device or applicator.

Avoid contact with open wounds.

Do not read this poem for persistent or chronic cough.

If symptoms persist for more than seven days, discontinue reading this poem and consult your doctor.

Do not place this poem in any container in which you are heating water.

Do not apply this poem to broken or irritated skin.

In case of serious burns or animal bites, do not read this poem. Consult a hospital.

If you are pregnant or nursing a baby, seek the advice of a health-care worker before reading this poem.

This poem has not been evaluated by the Food and Drug Administration. This poem is not intended to diagnose, treat, cure, or prevent any disease.

This poem is not intended for weight reduction.

A very small percentage of readers may develop a sensitivity to this poem. This sensitivity may result in an allergic reaction.

This poem may contain nuts or nut fragments.

This poem contains caffeine.

This poem contains phenylketonurics which contains phenylalanine.

This poem contains 21–28.7 percent mercury. Reading it may cause serious mercury poisoning.

This poem contains saccharine, which has been determined to cause cancer in laboratory animals.

This poem contains nicotine, known to cause birth defects.

Read this poem only in well-ventilated areas.

Avoid fire, flame, or smoking while reading this poem.

As with most poems, electrical parts of this poem are electrically live even when the poem is not being read. To reduce risk of death, always unplug poem after use.

Do not read while bathing.

Do not place or store where poem can fall or be pulled into tub, toilet, or sink.

If this poem falls into water, do not reach into water to retrieve it.

This poem may explode or leak and cause burn injury if disposed of in fire, mixed with poems of different types, or disassembled.

This poem contains liquid and vapors that may ignite.

Never spray and pull poems apart at the same time as this action creates static, which in itself is an electrical charge that could possibly ignite.

Do not puncture this poem.

Do not attempt to iron this poem or any poem while it is being worn on a body.

Do not read in temperatures above 120 degrees Fahrenheit as poem may burst.

Do not attempt to drive or operate heavy machinery while reading this poem.

Deliberately concentrating and inhaling the contents of this poem can be harmful or fatal.

Read only as directed. Entering this poem into the ear canal could cause injury.

The red tip is to remind you not to put this poem in your eye. If accidental contact with eyes occurs, immediately put down this poem and flush eyes with water.

Do not read more than three times a day.

For external use only. If rash develops, discontinue reading.

Avoid reading this poem if you have skin prone to spider veins and/or skin that is
     sensitive to peel-off face masks.
If the reading of this poem is accompanied by fever, headache, swelling, nausea, or
     vomiting, stop reading immediately.

Do not read to children under twelve years of age.
Supervise any children over six who read poems.
For children under two, use only a pea-sized amount of this poem.
Consult your pediatrician before reading to children under six months.
Keep poem away from babies' noses and mouths.
Keep this and all poems out of the reach of children.
The reading of this poem does not enable you to fly.

Love Which Took Its Symmetry for Granted

I was fidgeting with the radio dials. On Tuesdays this semester, Nick drops me off at FIU early and heads south, then picks me up after his second class at University of Miami. We were driving to work when we heard about the first plane going into one of the Twin Towers. I still thought it was a small plane, some horrible accident. Nick was running late, so I hopped out of the car while the announcer was explaining what she was seeing. I always stand at the curb for a minute as Nick eases into traffic and I wave goodbye.

>>At first I thought it was an earthquake. I ran to Gina's desk and said,
>>"Hurry up. We have to get out of here." She tried to make a joke.
>>"That's it! I'm handing in my resignation."

>>I was on 6th Ave., running late for work, when the first plane passed.
>>I will always associate that first image with the Tommy Hilfiger logo,
>>which was on a billboard in the foreground of my line of sight.

>>I am on 5th Street, about a mile just north of the World
>>Trade Center. Outside my living room window are some
>>low buildings in the foreground, opening to a clear view
>>of the north side of the upper forty floors of the Twin Towers.

>>Our apartment, on the tenth floor of the highest
>>building on the west side of Washington Square
>>Park, has always had an amazing view of the Twin Towers.

>>I was in Manhattan when the event occurred, but at a safe distance. I had gone in to
>>teach my morning class at FIT (on the West Side, 27th Street at 7th Avenue, about a
>>mile from the site.) I actually saw one of the towers on fire out the window before it
>>collapsed.

>>I heard the low-flying plane, sounding as though it
>>was just skimming the tops of the park's trees.

Most of us have known this for some time and expected some kind of significant attacks within the U.S. But now the genie is out of the bottle—and in a most spectacular fashion.

On September 10, 2001, these were my worries:

1. My dad, who collapsed at home and was admitted to the hospital.

2. Getting all the papers together to refinance our condo since the rates were going down to 6.325. We'd financed a year ago, when the rates were 8.125.

3. Gaining weight. I'd had a heel spur for over two weeks, two cortisone shots right into the foot. I couldn't exercise, except to swim. And it hurt a lot to walk on bare feet on the tiles around the pool.

Leslie A. Whittington, Georgetown University professor of public policy, perished with her husband and two daughters on AA flight 77.

How easy was our failure
to recognize the new weapon of the Middle East,
which neither Americans nor any other Westerners
could equal: the despair-driven, desperate suicide bomber.

There was a small black-and-white TV in a professor's office. The English department secretaries got a key and we watched both towers collapse, one after another, in grainy black and white. It was like a Godzilla movie. I kept leaving the room to do a bit of work—back and forth—I went to the bookstore downstairs to check that all the books for my class had come in, I put out some mail, I tried to read some student poems. I called my dad in the hospital, who said, "Oh my God, they just got the Pentagon." His heart, I kept thinking, his heart. So much easier to focus on one beloved heart.

>>Gina and I went down the stairs holding hands. I tried to call Eric but
>>my cell phone wouldn't work.

>>I was very concerned about how to get home,
>>especially since (as some of you know)
>>I'm expecting a baby girl and am now
>>three weeks from my due date.

Osama's mother, a Syrian beauty, was his father's fourth, and final, official wife . . .
she was considered by the conservative bin Laden family to be far ahead of her time.
(For instance, she refused to wear a burka over her Chanel suits when she traveled
abroad.)

>>A few bodegas are open.

>>*USS Cole*

What are the new implications of this new situation for our attitude and strategies
toward war and peace, how do we distinguish between the government's overbroad
definition of terrorism and actual terrorism?

>>Gina said that a prop plane must have hit the building. But I clung to
>>my earthquake theory. I wanted to believe Mother Nature was at fault.
>>When an injured employee was taken down the stairs, we were
>>told to hold ourselves flat against the wall. This guy went by on a
>>stretcher. His face was one big blister.

>>Balducci's opened, a surreal abundance on its grocery shelves with an occasional
>>reminder: no bananas, for example—no truck.

Indeed, who could ever point the finger at Americans now for using that pejorative and sometimes racist word "terrorism"?

I got my heel spur by pushing too hard. It was too hot in Florida to take my walks in July and August, so every day I got on the treadmill for an hour, a bowl of sweat under my neck and spreading to my shoulders. I really wanted to lose weight. I started doing the hills, the steep ones, and alternated watching the green digital calorie counter and the ladies of The View *on the hanging TV. Sometimes when an exerciser got there before me and watched something else, I'd put on my headphones and turn to a heavy-metal station and run as fast as I could. Sometimes I'd get these sharp pains in my calf, but I thought that was good. "Did you stretch?" the podiatrist asked. I was no longer young if I had a podiatrist, but he tried to cheer me and said, "Think of this as sports medicine. You know who had a heel spur? Larry Bird."*

Bin Laden was born in 1957,
the seventh son of fifty children
born to a Yemeni father who made millions
running construction projects in Saudi Arabia.

>>I've had some very strange dreams . . . September 12,
>>toward morning, I dreamed a woman with a Brooklyn or
>>Queens accent, in her twenties, was talking to me . . . she
>>said "Hello!" in a loud, clear voice. It woke me up. I
>>thought, who is this? I don't know anyone with this voice.
>>And then I realized . . . it was one of the missing WTC
>>workers. Maybe someone from Cantor Fitzgerald, 104th floor.
>>She was dead. And she didn't know she was dead.

34

You may wish to use some or all of your class time today for a discussion of yesterday and the unfolding tragedy:

>>a damp-fireplace smell began filling the apartment

Ask the class to establish ground rules for the discussion.

>>some people passing on the street with medical masks

1. Avoid blame and speculation.

>>Then I squeezed onto the packed train to Long Island. I was very
>>nervous about public transportation. What if someone blew up the
>>*train?*

2. Where you can, explore links to the content of your class or discipline.

>>When we were first dating Eric gave me this lucky crystal he bought on
>>the street in Soho. I always kept it on my desk. I left it behind in the
>>tower.

3. It's OK for students to share personal stories and feelings. (Be prepared for students to be emotional, and try to support and comfort them.)

>>We went out this morning.
>>No newspapers, no open stores.

4. Give students a chance to write before speaking.

>>An intercom message urged the employees to stay calm
>>and that there was no need to evacuate the building.

5. Respect each other's views and avoid inflammatory language.

>>I am aware of several likely fatalities,
>>including a police officer who knew
>>the entire set of beat cops for Precinct One
>>who are all gone, and my coworker Enid's
>>close friend Esra . . .

6. Ask students: in what ways are we affected by these events?

Word for the day, September 14, 2001
Knickerbocker (NIK-ehr BOHK-ehr) noun

1. A descendant of the Dutch settlers of New York.

2. A New Yorker.

[After Diedrich Knickerbocker, fictitious author of Washington Irving's (1783–1859) History of New York (1809).]

7. Ask the class: what hopes and fears do you have for this discussion?

>>My thoughts immediately went to the folks in the deli I joke
>>with when I get my morning coffee, the ladies in the bread
>>store where I get Warren's favorite bread, the people in
>>Borders bookstore, and the security guards . . .

8. Exchange ideas and strategies with other instructors, including debriefing the class discussion.

On the fourth of July in 2001, I went to throw something away in the garbage under the sink and there were chewed-up pieces of cantaloupe strewn everywhere, as though someone had vomited melon, as though—my first thought—our garbage disposal spun out of control. There were drying seeds and wet orange flecks on the bottles of Glass Plus, Comet, Drano, the balled-up Publix bags we always keep, just in case. I called my husband to take a look, semi-blaming him, asking, "Did you put melon into the disposal?" He crouched and looked and found two gnawed holes on the bottom of our garbage bag, which hangs on the inside of the door under our sink. We both knew it was a rat, maybe several rats. The hair on my arms was in alert. I said we have to go get traps. We spent our July fourth plugging up holes with Brillo pads and duct tape, setting our strategic glue traps (the cruelest traps of all) in the kitchen against the wall. It took two days to get it. The first night we found one trap covered in hair and blood, which meant the rat stepped on it but at great pain to itself, rolled or leapt off. But night two it was there, straining and pulling with tiny screams. My husband flipped it into a Tupperware container, a makeshift grave. Buried it alive by snapping the lid. Our fear was such that he taped it shut. It was very heavy to pick up. I felt no guilt the way I'd felt guilt with trapping mice when we lived in NY. I felt instead victory and relief. We still keep a glue trap under the sink. I never would have guessed there were rats in Florida. Palmetto bugs yes, lizards yes. But rats?

"Wherever we look, we find the U.S. as the leader of terrorism and crime in the world."

—Osama bin Laden

Fare	Coach Class From:	To:
$152	Boston, MA (BOS)	New Orleans, LA (MSY)
$79	Indianapolis, IN (IND)	St. Louis, MO (STL)
$159	St. Louis, MO (STL)	Austin, TX (AUS)
$129	St. Louis, MO (STL)	Sioux Falls, SD (FSD)

>>Pete works in the Federal Building, only a few blocks away. He went
>>downstairs to get his usual coffee and chocolate donut from Abdoul, the vendor
>>who parks his cart outside. So Pete stood on the steps, sipping his
>>coffee, etc. when he heard a whizzing noise, looked up, and saw a plane flying
>>very low . . . too low. Then he saw it crash into Tower One. His instincts told
>>him, Get out of here—don't go back upstairs, back to work . . . he started
>>walking . . . all the way home to Astoria. It took him five hours.

>>Joanne is upset and believes more carnage is on the way.
>>I don't think anything will happen too quickly . . .

Theology versus technology, the suicide bomber against nuclear power.

Tuesday, at about 6 p.m., Michael calls from LA to ask how I am. We both bemoan our beloved NY. We both feel so helpless, now living so far away. Then he says, "I know this is tacky—but do you think there were any celebrities on the flights? I mean, the planes were all headed for CA."

Mari-Rae Sopper, newly hired women's gymnastics coach at University of California, Santa Barbara, who was making the trip to start her new job on flight AA 77.

>>I wish I were younger and trained in armaments. I would like
>>to be La Femme Nikita and just take out this billionaire jerk.
>>He's tall, thin, smart, good looking, charismatic, and rich.
>>Sort of like the fuck ups I fall for anyway, except for the
>>latter financial issue.

>>Denise, here's a paraphrasing of what Madonna said at the Staples Center Thursday
>>night: Any of you who purchased a ticket to the show tonight will be contributing
>>to a fund that will be for children orphaned by this tragedy, so thank you all. Now
>>on a personal note I think that each and every one of us should look inside our own
>>hearts and examine our own personal acts of terrorism, hatred, intolerance,
>>negativity, the list goes on and on, we're all responsible. It's not just bin Laden, it's

>>all of us, we've all contributed to hatred in the world today. And I would like to
>>have one minute of silence to say a prayer for those who have died; to pray for the
>>friends and families of those who have died; to say a prayer for the rescuers who
>>have worked night and day to rescue people from the rubble. And most of all say a
>>prayer for anyone who thinks that it is right to kill in the name of God. Where
>>there is violence, there is no God. Let's have a moment of silence. Hold hands with
>>those around you. Or stay still and reflect.

. . . a man known as the Good Samaritan or the Saudi Prince.
He would arrive unannounced, it was said, at hospitals
where wounded Afghan and Arab fighters had been brought.
He was lean and elegant, and dressed in the traditional
shalwar kameez of the Afghan tribes—a blousy knee-length
tunic top—over tailored trousers of fine English cloth . . . he was
soft-spoken, and went from bed to bed dispensing cashews and
English chocolates to the wounded. . . . Weeks later, the man's family
would receive a generous check. . . . This man also turned out
to be bin Laden.

>>Pete stopped with a small crowd of people and saw the second plane hit Tower
>>Two. Then he was back on the walk . . .

>>Gordon immediately started to bolt down the stairs by twos and threes
>>or more, afraid for his life. When he approached approximately the
>>20th floor, the stairway was crowded with people who were moving

>>more slowly, but he said they were remarkably orderly and calm,
>>following the directives given by the fire marshals in charge.

Bin Laden's genius for self-promotion

>>No schools, no mail service, no subway service,
>>no non-emergency traffic; police check IDs
>>when pedestrians try to cross the line, to make
>>sure you reside or have business in the area.

FBI's Ten Most Wanted List since 1993

>>The lumps in our stomachs left no room for food.

Cindy and I go to give blood at the mall, but it's a two-hour wait. A guy with a clipboard says, "Go shopping in the meantime," but neither one of us wants to go shopping. Plus my foot really hurts, but it feels too small to complain about that in the face of everything else.

>>We are afraid too, and the TV and radio are open all the day!
>>It's uncredable!

>>But i'm sure that we are going to find those horible poeple!
>>Courage, we are with you!!!!!
>>I will contact you later because I'm going to do the genealogy
>>of the Duhamel.
>>—Laetitia Duhamel from France

Jane's Intelligence Review's definition of Al-Qaeda: a conglomerate of groups
spread throughout the world operating as a network. It has a global
reach, with a presence in Algeria, Egypt, Morocco, Turkey,

When I call my loan officer, he wants to know if I still want to work with him. His name is Abad. I say, "yes," feeling kind of guilty, thinking maybe it's crass to proceed with the mortgage. I only get it when he says—"a lot of people have asked to switch, to work with someone else."

Jordan,
Tajikistan, Uzbekistan, Syria, Xinjiang in China, Pakistan, Bangladesh, Malaysia,
Myanmar, Indonesia, Mindanao in the Philippines,

>>haven't been able to get online since
>>tues. first time. and got yr sweet phone msg also.
>>like an armed camp right now. cops on every corner.
>>candlelight vigils, vespers. but also beautiful
>>weather & no cars south of 14th st, so there's this

>>bucolic feel as well—kids on skates etc. grief & just
>>plain joy at being alive i guess.

                                    Lebanon, Iraq, Saudi
Arabia, Kuwait, Bahrain, Yemen, Libya,

"I wish I was in NY," Michael says. "I'd go down to St. Vincent's and say, 'Put me to work.'"

                              Tunisia, Bosnia, Kosovo,
Chechnya, Dagestan, Kashmir, Sudan, Somalia, Kenya, Tanzania,
Azerbaijan, Eritrea, Uganda, Ethiopia, and in the West Bank and Gaza.

>>He might have positioned himself to fall headfirst, my husband
>>suggested, because he wanted to ensure that he die on impact.

>>I watched TV all night. Around three in the morning, the
>>cat tipped over a bottle of shampoo which thudded on
>>the bathroom floor. I started screaming. Eric starting
>>screaming. The cat zoomed under the bed.

two U.S. embassies in Africa in 1998

About two hours before the planes hit the Twin Towers, I went to the American Airlines Web site to buy a ticket to go see my dad over the weekend. I felt really far away and small. I was knocked offline just as I was putting in my credit card number for the Miami-Logan Weekend Saver. I was frustrated so I thought I'd wait and do it at school where the computer hookup to the net is faster.

Tutors and nannies, bearers and butlers formed a large part of his life. He and his half brothers—and, to a lesser extent, his thirty half sisters—were playmates of the children of the kingdom's most prominent families . . .

>>This is to let you know that Sam arrived home safe
>>and sound tonight from the World Trade Center ordeal.
>>His office was on the 78th floor of Tower Two.

The bank account statements we need for our refinancing are lost in the mail. I'm on the phone for hours with Christian, the branch manager. His name looks very strange as I write it on a post-it.

Was it an intelligence failure or a policy failure? Or both?

How do we break the fragmentation, disorganization,
and isolation of the left under these harsh conditions?

*The rats were coming into our building, the exterminator said, because they'd been displaced
by the digging for a new hotel up the street. Rats have a huge roaming range—we're eight
buildings away.*

He now has four wives, carefully chosen for their political
connections or their pedigree, and some ten children.

>>Working on 18th Street on the West Side, Warren was on the roof of
>>his building and saw the plane head for and deliberately fly into
>>Tower One. He ran down the stairs, called me completely out of breath.

"Break a vase, and the love that reassembles the fragments
is stronger than the love which took its symmetry for
granted when it was whole."—Derek Walcott

I kept asking Marta, the English department secretary, "What day is it today?" September 11. September 11. Is that a significant date in history? I didn't know about Camp David. I didn't know until I filled out a green duplicating form at school—9/11 and I paused and saw it before I wrote "01."

Al-Qaeda may have received training and financial assistance
from the CIA, helping create a hard-line Islamic Frankenstein
from which the U.S. would later recoil.

Daniel C. Lewin, doctoral student at MIT and cofounder of Akamai
Technologies Inc., a company that helps relieve congestion on the
Internet, on flight AA 11.

USA Today reported that bin Laden
uses digital encryption tools to hide messages
in typical Web pornography and sports chat discussions.
These messages may very well include plans
for upcoming terrorist attacks.

The doctor says if the shots don't work, we'll get you a blue boot to wear all the time. It's like the splint you wear at night, but you'll have to wear it round the clock for six weeks. I'm doing everything I can to avoid the twenty-four-hour puffy fashion disaster boot. Extra ice. Dr. Scholl's heel pads.

"The abortionists have got to bear some burden for this because God will not be mocked. And when we destroy forty million little innocent babies, we make God mad. I really believe that the pagans, and the abortionists, and the feminists, and the gays and lesbians who are actively trying to make that an alternative lifestyle, the ACLU, People for the American Way—all of them who have tried to secularize America—I point the finger in their face and say, 'You helped this happen.'"—Jerry Falwell

I find all my friends—it takes three days—everyone's OK, though they've almost all lost someone. One guy who works on the 102nd floor oversleeps fifteen minutes. "Survival of the slackest" is the joke, but not until Friday night. That's the first "joke."

>>This old guy was fast, like a mountain goat. He called down
>>the stairs, "Come on! I'm faster than the lot of you and I have
>>an artificial hip!" Gina started to laugh which made everyone
>>else laugh too. She kept digging her fingernails into my hand.

I called my dad just as he was about to get communion. I called my dad just as he was being wheeled down into x-ray. I called my dad when he wasn't in his bed.

>>Then a moment of silence, but several morons kept screaming "We love you,
>>Madonna" at which point she said "Shut Up!" and then there was actually an arena

>>full of silent Madonna fans. Several people around me were crying and it was a very
>>intimate, touching moment.

My dad could have had: a heart attack, a stroke, or a heart-related problem caused by a low pulse.

"With small capabilities, and with our faith, we can defeat the greatest
military power of modern times. America is much weaker than it appears."
—bin Laden

>>Do you think Americans will lose interest as regular
>>programming comes back on TV? They better keep showing
>>that rubble until there's some war footage . . .

>>Then Madonna climbed the stairs to sing "Secret," but first said "And one more thing:
>>If you want to change the world, you must first start with yourself." "Secret" seemed
>>to have a lot of new meaning and she sang a very heartfelt rendition of it.

I received my first merit raise on Tuesday. The notice was in my school mail. I forgot to tell Nick until the next day.

He operates more as a venture capitalist of terror
than a military leader, disbursing funds to a loose network
of terrorists and operatives scattered around the world.

>>My young neighbor was coming up the stairs, dressed in
>>her tattered power suit and in complete shock.

"You will not die needlessly. Your lives are in the hands of God."—bin Laden

Robert G. LeBlanc, emeritus professor of cultural geography at the
University of New Hampshire, Durham, on United 175.

>>When we finally made it down all the stairs in Tower One, we still had
>>to go down an escalator that was also covered with water. The
>>escalators weren't moving. It was hard to see where the steps began
>>and ended. There was a policeman at the bottom trying to catch the
>>people who were slipping.

*We're numb Wednesday and Thursday. "We should have bought a paper," Nick says. And I
picture all those* New York Posts *and* Time *magazines in plastic sleeves at flea markets
twenty-five years from now.*

49

>>He came home, briefly, and was watching through binoculars beside me when
>>the second one fell.

>>They had to rinse out his eyes.

>>I turned, jumped up, and grabbed my binoculars and saw red
>>fire inside a number of floors.

>>Hundreds of students were evacuated from dormitories south of 14th
>>Street, and have since been without clothing or books; those who
>>couldn't double up with someone are now sleeping on cots at NYU's
>>mammoth gym.

We were looking for Time *or* Newsweek *everywhere yesterday, but they were all sold out. I finally slept a whole night, so I feel a little less helpless. Also, yesterday I did that light-a-candle-at-7 p.m.-thing. Nick and I were at Publix, running late as usual, so I bought a votive candle and went outside. I felt really silly thinking that I was going to be there alone, but suddenly there were about twenty of us—and more in front of other stores in the strip mall—and the most amazing thing happened. It had been raining, then at 7 o'clock there was a huge double rainbow in the sky. We all started crying. It was really cool. I've been wanting to go to church, and that seemed churchy and healing.*

how to respond to an enemy who is a man and not a state;
who has no structured organization, no headquarters, and no fixed address

>>Once I worked on the 103rd floor of the World Trade Center.
>>For three and a half years, I spent most of my waking hours there.
>>Some evenings, working late, dusk would fall and the city skyline
>>would appear like diamonds against black velvet. On one fourth
>>of July, I returned there to watch fireworks; from my vantage point
>>of being so high up in the tower, the fireworks seemed to explode
>>directly in front of my face.

In 1968, Osama's father (along with his American pilot)
died in a helicopter crash, and Osama, at the age of thirteen,
inherited eighty million dollars.

My dad had the best of the three options—his low pulse had affected his heart. He was going to get a pacemaker—even a better model than Dick Cheney's, his doctor said. "Oh good, I'll be able to send you a fax through it," I said, stealing David Letterman's joke about the vice president's pacemaker.

>>On the photograph, note, too, how the blood on the man's
>>shirt is clearly discernible, despite that the photo is
>>black and white. Can you see the color red with me? It
>>seems to me that when you are a poet looking at

>>something, you need to see beyond what is visible. So:
>>can you see the color red with me?

>>Gerry does now have power back, and water . . .

The day I woke up with my spur, I couldn't put any weight on my right foot at all. None. I had to crawl to the bathroom. I learned quickly that I really didn't know how to hop on one foot, especially my left.

>>Tonight I will do laundry, and read a book. And pray.

Karen Kinkaid, a new adjunct professor, School of Law, Catholic University, on flight AA 77.

"A Klee painting named 'Angelus Novus'
shows an angel looking as though he is about
to move away from something he is fixedly
contemplating. His eyes are staring,
his mouth is open, his wings are spread.
This is how one pictures the angel of history.
His face is turned toward the past.
Where we perceive a chain of events,

he sees one single catastrophe which
keeps piling wreckage upon wreckage
and hurls it in front of his feet.
The angel would like to stay, awaken the dead,
and make whole what has been smashed.
But a storm is blowing from Paradise;
it has got caught in his wings with such violence
that the angel can no longer close them.
This storm irresistibly propels him into the future
to which his back is turned, while the pile of debris
before him grows skyward. This storm
is what we call progress."—Walter Benjamin

*On Friday, my dad tries to go home from the hospital, but he's bleeding around his pacemak-
er. He has really thin blood from the medicine he takes. His dressing is all pink, like the blood
of rare meat.*

It is no longer theoretical.

>>You ask what it feels like here . . . World War I?
>>The beginning of World War III? The Middle Ages?
>>All different time periods, jumbled together.
>>Three blocks from my apartment, on Ditmars, near
>>the subway stop, is a long row of candles,
>>drawings, and pictures of Christ.

>>Then water began gushing from behind us. Gina and I tried to keep
>>our balance, always staying on the same step, like a pair trying to make
>>it to Noah's Ark. The water was ankle deep and pushed off our pumps.
>>Then we saw Stacey. Stacey held Theo's hand. Gina held onto mine.

The Accident

(September 10, 2003)

The escalator is going up,
my father behind my mother, one stair down.
Jack and Jill go up
the silver, jagged hill, up
the crowded escalator. My parents fall—
up is down, down is up,
and no one is left standing up
anymore, the metal steps,
the howling hungry steps
with mean metal teeth, rip up
my mother's white jeans, leave Twister-size blood
spots. Her white sneakers streaked with bloody

stripes. Her khaki purse speckled with bloody
polka dots. Her favorite sweater, shredded, torn up.
The Band-Aid in her purse, sopped in blood.
Her money, her credit cards, smudged with blood.
Jack comes tumbling down—
my father's hand is stripped of skin. His blood
mixes with my mother's blood, blood
brother, blood sister. Jill comes tumbling. A waterfall,
her crown of hair caught in the steps. Flung pails, a bloodfall.
My mother needs two blood
transfusions. The doctors step
into her crisis. My father steps

over a stranger's body to look for my mother, steps
with a towel around his hand to help clot his bloody
fingers. An EMT worker steps

toward my mother, steps
toward her, though he is afraid he will throw up—
she looks that bad. He takes steps
to stop the bleeding, steps
to put her head, her crown of hair, back on. Down
goes my father. When he sees my mother, he goes down.
He is fainting, his heart is beating out of step.
The towel around his hand falls
to the ground. His glasses fall

to the orange carpet, the carpet the color of fall
leaves. My mother is a blur to him. I step
toward the phone, the doctor calling about the fall.
I fall into the wall, then fall
into crisis mode, unprepared for the hospital—all the blood
and bruising, all the stitches that don't fall
into any pattern I can figure out. My parents' fallow
cheeks. Witnesses say a fifteen-person pileup,
my mother on the bottom—the steps going up
collapse, then zoom backwards, falling
into reverse. My father screams in his flimsy gown, down-
the-up-staircase, up-the-down-

staircase nightmares. He used to sing to us, *Down
in the bottom of an itty-bitty pool* . . . Now he can't fall
asleep without falling, down
in the bottom of his own big pool of blood, down
into his dream in which the moving steps
still pull him, still pull my mother down.
Blood runs down
my mother's forehead, blood
runs into her eyes. She wipes the blood

away to see my father go down
and crawl toward her, curl up
around her. The doctor stitches my mother up,

pulls the skin of her scalp back up,
but her blood pressure is way down,
down and falling
to fifty over nothing. My father steps
up the hill to fetch another pail of blood.

Möbius Strip: Forgetfulness

                    she tries
to pee in the trash can but
misses   she puts
her socks over her
shoes   she wears
all her necklaces at
once   she has
another bruise   she
hides her rings in the
toaster slots   she
shoves the toast in the
VCR   she holds
the Chili's menu upside-
down   she tries to
eat an acorn   she
likes to eat canned
frosting   she is
small and curled on
the bed   she forgets
her underwear   she
feeds her stuffed dog so
its mouth is sticky with
chocolate   she's sure
the hippopotamus on TV
is real   sometimes
she can still say "Sprite"
or "Coke"   someone
sticks her thumb into
ink   she stacks
m&m's like ammunition

in her silver lipstick
tube   she holds
her plastic fork by the
tines   someone
pushes down her thumb
on the signature line
for a thumbprint   her
bright costume necklaces
jangle   she doesn't
recognize the baby
anymore   someone
is telling her to lift her
arms   someone is
telling her she has to
sing   she waters
the silk lilies   she
waters the silk lilies with
orange juice   she
waters the silk lilies
with milk   she
tries to write something
down with a spoon   she
forgets her wig   some-
times she can still say
"papa"   she can't
open her closet since
they locked it   at
three a.m. she leaves the
hotel room to wander
the beige carpeted
halls   she looks
at pink mums as

though she's about to
cry   all the room
numbers are a twisting
ruckus and what's her
name anyway   the
front desk clerk finds
her curled on a lobby
couch, pee wetting her
thin nightgown   the
orderly finds her curled
on the floor of someone
else's room, pee wetting
her thin nightgown
again   she doesn't
recognize Jesus   her
husband is upset by the
middle-of-the-night call—
yes please thank you please
bring her back   her
husband is upset by the
middle-of-the-night call—
yes please thank you I'll be
right there   she
plops a can of Campbell's
soup in the toilet
bowl   the bottom
of her sock drawer
is lined with melted
m&m's   she doesn't
want to kiss Jesus's
feet   she can't
smell anything, good

or bad   she uses
her lipstick as eye-
shadow   she
loses her favorite
crucifix   she
carries an empty
pocketbook   she
doesn't recognize
the pudding   she
doesn't recognize her
son   she wears a
baseball cap she stole
from another Alzheimer's
patient   she turns
on the stove to watch
the flames   she
wears her sweater as a
hat   she turns on
the stove to touch the
blue flowers   she
tries to eat a checker, then
a domino   she plops
a can of Chicken of
the Sea tuna in the toilet
bowl   she falls out
of bed   she folds
the same towel over and
over   where's her
little dog

Embarazar

The Dairy Association's huge success with the campaign "Got Milk?" prompted them to expand advertising to Mexico. It was soon brought to their attention that the Spanish translation read, "Are you lactating?" This worries me because I am in Spain and my period is over a week late. *Café con leche descafienado con sacarina, por favor.* You're not supposed to have swordfish when you're pregnant, so I order it. My body refuses to give me a hint. I feel no premenstrual bloating, no breast swelling, no backache. I feel no morning sickness, no cravings. I feel my stomach for signs of a heartbeat. I imagine my breasts, spilling over with *leche. When Parker marketed a ballpoint pen in South America, its ads were supposed to have read, "It won't leak in your pocket and embarrass you." The company thought that the word "embarazar" (to impregnate) meant to embarrass, so the ad read: "It won't leak in your pocket and make you pregnant!"* I fear my husband's pen has leaked into my pocket. I look at my calendar figuring out when I can schedule an abortion once we get home. I wonder if we should drive up to France, where I'm pretty sure I could find RU486, the French Abortion Pill, which, if it's ever marketed in the United States, will be called Mifepristone. Or I wonder if we should keep the baby (who would come in January) and figure out a place to fit a crib in the apartment. Today we saw a Down's syndrome girl on the bus biting her arm. I'll be forty by the time the baby comes. *Frank Perdue's chicken slogan, "It takes a tough man to make a tender chicken," was translated into Spanish as "it takes an aroused man to make a chicken affectionate."* My husband has been aroused a lot lately, like Frank. We are on vacation, which makes me affectionate. I want to buy one of those little pregnancy test kits, but it is Sunday so all the *farmacias* are closed. My husband has always been careful about putting a cap on his pen, and I have always been diligent in making sure he does, but now I remember that one awful time that we were so in a hurry doing laundry that one of our Papermates turned a whole batch of whites blue.

Lawless Pantoum

Men are legally allowed to have sex with animals,
as long as the animals are female.
Having sexual relations with a male animal
is taboo and punishable by death.

As long as the fish are female
saleswomen in tropical fish stores are allowed to go topless.
Adultery is punishable by death
as long as the betrayed woman uses her bare hands to kill her husband.

Saleswomen in tropical fish stores are allowed to go topless,
but the gynecologist must only look at a woman's genitals in a mirror.
The woman uses her bare hands to kill her husband,
then his dead genitals must be covered with a brick.

The gynecologist must only look at a woman's genitals in a mirror
and never look at the genitals of a corpse—
these genitals must be covered with a brick.
The penalty for masturbation is decapitation.

A look at the genitals of a corpse
will confirm that not much happens in that region after death.
The penalty for masturbation is decapitation.
It is illegal to have sex with a mother and her daughter at the same time.

To confirm what happens during sex,
a woman's mother must be in the room to witness her daughter's deflowering,
though it is illegal to have sex with a mother and her daughter at the same time.
It is legal to sell condoms from vending machines as long as

a woman's mother is in the room to witness her daughter's deflowering.
Men are legally allowed to have sex with animals—
why it's even legal to sell condoms from vending machines, as long as
everyone's having sexual relations with a male animal.

from *Mille et un sentiments*

(after Hervé Le Tellier's *Mille pensées*)

1. I feel as though something is terribly wrong.
2. I feel as though when I try to explain myself, I'm even less understood.
3. I feel excited by the thought of a tree crashing down right in front of me so that I'd have to stop, step over it, and leave my car behind.
4. I feel as though I'm too old now for an eyebrow ring.
5. I feel happy whenever you leave.
6. I feel hungry around four in the afternoon.
7. I feel silly admitting that I don't know the governor's name.
8. I feel ashamed that I don't know the capitals of certain states.
9. I feel like banging a hammer into her solar plexus when she whines.
10. I feel like having a good fight.
11. I feel like having a bad cry.
12. I feel like the bad guy when you look at me that way.
13. I feel insecure around scientists.
14. I feel insecure around dentists.
15. I feel sometimes like my parents are looking through the window when I write, even though they live in another city.
16. I feel like taking an eye bath.
17. I feel like using the lazy tongs tonight.
18. I feel as though you've got to hate with dignity, you've got to hate as though your whole life depends on it—or maybe someone just told me that in a dream.
19. I feel happiest in New York.
20. I feel creepy when I see that baby woodchuck caught in the fox's mouth.
21. I feel frustrated when the phone company changes the area code.
22. I feel as though they first talk my ears off, then my whole face off, chewing up my torso and limbs, until I am just a little pair of feet trying to run away.
23. I feel hardly anything when I see homeless people anymore, especially if I am in a hurry.
24. I feel drunk when I spend too much money.

25. I feel road rage and supermarket cart rage, especially when I get the cart with the dragging wheel. Why doesn't someone fix those things or throw them out?
26. I feel guilty when I don't bicycle.
27. I feel my spine curl up like a jump rope before I get hit.
28. I feel like something metaphorical is being said when the flight attendant tells us to put on our own oxygen masks before assisting small children with theirs.
29. I feel as though I've probably said the word fag when I shouldn't have.
30. I feel as though everyone should pay more attention to me.
31. I feel like a failure when I don't fill my quota.
32. I feel jealous of the lilacs that just hang there while everyone coos and comes to sniff them.
33. I feel like having another drink.
34. I feel as though my dreams aren't telling me enough.
35. I feel as though I don't even trust the process of writing anymore.
36. I feel as though only writing can save me.
37. I feel as though I need to be saved from something, but what? (Born Agains, please don't get the wrong idea.)
38. I feel happiest in a movie theater.
39. I feel shallow and full at the same time, you know?
40. I feel paranoid, as though my bedroom window is a TV screen.
41. I feel my breasts for lumps.
42. I feel like having lobster for dinner.
43. I feel strongly about gun control.
44. I feel depressed whenever I think about the TV special on Johannesburg—one out of four women having been raped.
45. I feel as though I'd rather be killed than be raped.
46. I feel like rape is killing.
47. I feel as though I may lose my male audience when I list such things.
48. I feel conflicted about being attracted to him, in particular.
49. I feel threatened by certain men.
50. I feel lucky to be an organ donor.

51. I feel squeamish about being cut open after I'm dead because of this dream I had as a little kid in which the dead could still feel things, but mostly I feel OK.
52. I feel hopeful about next year.
53. I feel hopeless when it comes to losing weight.
54. I feel hip when I think about flying to Paris.
55. I feel scared alone in the big house.
56. I feel insecure on the beach.
57. I feel secure when he puts his legs over mine when we're falling asleep.
58. I feel as though my ankle is an anthill opening its roof when my foot falls asleep.
59. I feel elated when I'm alone in my room.
60. I feel the need to listen to certain music when getting dressed for a party.
61. I feel like black is the right color to wear.
62. I feel cranky a few days before my period.
63. I feel relieved when my period comes.
64. I feel men also have some kind of hormonal cycle.
65. I feel like I don't even believe in binary concepts anymore, like *men* and *women*.
66. I feel threatened by certain women though, I'll admit it.
67. I feel as though I should speak up when someone makes a sexist remark.
68. I feel guilty when I let a sexist remark go unchecked because I'm intimidated by the person who made it.
69. I feel like a big drag making politically correct statements.
70. I feel humorless—and not always in connection to #69.
71. I feel like shoplifting small things sometimes.
72. I feel angry at myself when I don't meet my goals.
73. I feel like no one even cares what my goals are but me.
74. I feel self-centered—I feel like putting on my favorite hat, the one that I designed myself, the one with the mirror hanging from its brim so I can constantly look into my own eyes.
75. I feel bad when he tells me I'm too self-centered.
76. I feel as though I should work more on being less self-centered.
77. I feel no more than 77 percent of any list poem should be autobiographical.
78. I feel as though no one respects me because I'm a go-go dancer.

79. I feel like being pushed against the wall, then spanked.

80. I feel like going topless everywhere—that's how much I like myself.

81. I feel as though if you knew I had both a penis and a vagina, you might not want to date me. Is this true?

82. I feel as though everyone should admire my Rolex.

83. I feel as though the Porsche we just bought might be a little too flashy.

84. I feel bad about that bank I vandalized with glue and puka shells.

85. I feel great about my new workout video. Do you like it?

86. I feel that my publicist doesn't really want you to know the real me.

87. I feel like I owe an apology to my fans about the Play Doh incident.

88. I feel like jumping out a first-floor window and breaking both of my ankles.

89. I feel as though no one understands my accent.

90. I feel slighted by the supermarket checkout person who still doesn't know my name.

91. I feel greedy, even when I eat only a carrot.

92. I feel as though the best friends I ever made I made in boot camp.

93. I feel that pop music really says it all.

94. I feel as though the cure for cancer is right around the corner.

95. I feel my mouth go dry in terror whenever I hear a cricket.

96. I feel proud and slightly arrogant when I give up sugar.

97. I feel bad about the bomb I dropped on your country—I pressed the wrong button.

98. I feel a surge of confidence whenever people laugh at me.

99. I feel your nipples, then go blind and they are braille.

100. I feel as though everything is going to be just fine.

. . .

401. I feel open to writing in general.

402. I feel open to free writing, sestinas, and haiku.

403. I feel open to sonnets and canzones, villanelles and pantoums.

404. I feel open to collages and centos.

405. I feel open to memory and my dreams.

406. I feel open to recipes and headlines and found poems of all kinds.

407. I feel open to nonsense and I feel open to sense.

408. I feel open to lists and inversions.

409. I feel open to squirting KY Jelly on my brain, if necessary, to get things going.

410. I feel open to reading the slaves.

411. I feel open to reading the masters.

412. I feel open to taking long walks and clustering.

413. I feel open to taking a nap to see what happens.

414. I feel open to mopping the floor, to see if the gray dreadlocks in soapy water remind me of Ophelia.

415. I feel open to revision and revisionist mythmaking.

416. I feel open to bribing the Muse.

417. I feel open to begging.

418. I feel open to melodrama and understatement.

419. I feel open to calling a friend and asking for advice.

420. I feel open to collaboration with children or adults.

421. I feel open to sulking.

422. I feel open to silkworms, the way they create no matter what.

423. I feel open to painting, knitting, making a cake.

424. I feel open to making anything at all.

425. I feel open to humiliation.

426. I feel like opening the dictionary just to look at some words: galaxy, cucumber, scissors, tintinnabulation.

427. I feel open to using these four words in a four-line stanza:
>   the cucumber peel in the sink was the first tipoff
>   that something was wrong—
>   then the terrible tintinnabulation of the galaxy
>   like scissors preening the fur of a small dog . . .

428. I feel open to poems within poems.

429. I feel open to giving away my secrets.

430. I feel open to looking like a fool.

431. I feel open to crumpling up what I've written.

432. I feel open to starting all over again.

433. I feel open to free fall and thudding.

434. I feel open to soaring.

435. I feel open to simile and metaphor.

436. I feel open to synecdoche, synesthesia, and sin.

437. I feel open to miracles and the mariachi.

438. I feel open to machismo, Mary Poppins, Milk Duds, and murder.

439. In other words, I feel open to alliteration.

440. I feel open to assonance as well.

441. I feel open to acting like an absolute ass.

442. I feel open to riding the back of an ass, if I can somehow get a poem out of it.

443. I feel open to sitting on my ass in front of the TV with the sound off to see if that sets off any sparks.

444. I feel open to writing about asses and their different shapes.

445. I feel open to my own desperation for new subject matter.

446. I even feel open to the fact that maybe there are already enough poems in the world.

447. I feel open to becoming a train conductor instead.

448. I feel open to specializing in yoga or suntans.

449. I feel open to getting out of my own head and learning to kickbox.

450. I feel open to going back to the Warhol Museum in Pittsburgh to see the punching bags Warhol made with Basquiat.

451. I feel open to punching bags decorated with the face of Christ.

452. I feel open to punching God just to see what it feels like.

453. I feel open to taboo.

454. I feel open to the international sign for toilets in Spain—a stick figure sitting on the can.

455. I feel open to being discreet.

456. I feel open to other international signs for toilets, the silhouette of a woman in a skirt or a man in pants.

457. I feel open to making a Play-Doh Garcia Lorca.

458. I feel open to doing Pablo Neruda's Etch A Sketch portrait.

459. I feel open to writing Sylvia Plath's name on a Lite-Brite board.

460. I feel open to cartwheels and Scrabble.

461. I feel open to using all the words from a finished Scrabble game in a poem.

462. I feel open to writing a poem using only words from the *Official Scrabble Dictionary*.

463. I feel open to rigor.

464. I feel open to cheating.

465. I feel open to misinterpretation and mistakes.

466. I feel open to the T-shirt in Miami promoting the Pope's visit. Instead of "I saw the Pope" (el Papa), the shirt read "I Saw the Potato" (la papa).

467. I feel open to seeing the Potato.

468. I feel open to the Holy Potato and its Holy Eyes.

469. I feel open to Mr. Potato Head dressed in a pope's gown.

470. I feel open to Mr. Potato Pope and his views on abortion.

471. I feel open to Pope Potato the Second.

472. I feel open to La Papa Segunda.

473. I feel open to as many languages as possible.

474. I feel open to translation.

475. I feel open to poems of political protest.

476. I feel open to prose poems and open to stanzas.

477. I feel open to couplets about chicken cutlets.

478. I feel open to terza rima about tiramisu.

479. I feel open to anecdotal poems about childhood.

480. I feel open to putting the names of poets in spell-check just to see what alternatives pop up.

481. I feel open to Dorianne Laux becoming Darwin Lax.

482. I feel open to Ai becoming Ax.

483. I feel open to Elizabeth Bishop, Molly Peacock, and Jean Valentine passing through spell-check unaltered.

484. I feel open to caesura. I feel open to lines that bleed onto the next.

485. I feel open to meter and counterpoint.

486. I feel open to landscape poems with sheep dots and goat spots and mountains that look like sleeping giants in profile.

487. I feel open to the small white milk teeth of first-graders and mentioning them in poems for good luck.

488. I feel open to mushrooms and mushroom clouds.

489. I feel open to clouds of smoke, clouds of dust, and clouds of pink cotton candy fuzz.

490. I feel open to ritual and magic.

491. I feel open to abstraction and the five senses.

492. I feel open to Mad Libs and liberation of all kinds.

493. I feel open to turning Oscar Wilde's famous quote into a Lescurean word square:

> All bad poetry springs from genuine feeling.
>
> All bad feelings spring from genuine poetry.
>
> All genuine poetry springs from bad feelings.
>
> All genuine feeling springs from bad poetry, etc.

494. I feel open to how the word look looks like "look," the two o's, two round open eyes.

495. I feel open to becoming a nonce word.

496. I feel open to my own goose bumps.

497. I feel open to the little stuck-up hairs on my arm.

498. I feel open to pushing an idea too far.

499. I feel open to holding back.

500. I feel open to closure and the lack of it.

. . .

801. I feel that, as a person caught between Generation X and the Baby Boomers, I've had a very hard time growing up.

802. I feel like this must be extremely annoying to others who have had no choice but to grow up.

803. I feel like I have grown up to a point, but I'm not as grown up as my parents were at my age.

804. I feel like I am happier, maybe, than they were.

805. I feel like there's no real way to be sure.

806. I feel as though I'm not as critical of TV as I should be.

807. I feel as though most recent TV shows—except for CNN, *Once and Again,* and *Talk Soup*—bore me.

808. I feel as though I don't really know TV anymore.

809. I feel out of it when people talk about the *X-Files* or *Party of Five.*

810. I feel as though all the young actresses look the same now.

811. I feel that I can't tell the difference between the singers either. What's the difference between Christina Aguilera and Britney Spears? Backstreet Boys or *NSYNC?

812. I feel as though I can usually, although not always, relate to the people I meet, even when their feelings differ from mine.

813. I feel as though I can usually, although not always, relate to characters on TV.

814. I feel, for instance, like Mary Hartman (Louise Lasser) on *Mary Hartman, Mary Hartman.*

815. I feel like Jan Brady (Eve Plumb) on *The Brady Bunch.*

816. I feel like Samantha Stephens (Elizabeth Montgomery) on *Bewitched.*

817. I feel like a contestant who goes home with only parting gifts on *Wheel of Fortune.*

818. I feel like J.J. (Jimmy Walker) on *Good Times.*

819. I feel like Danny (Danny Bonaduce) on *The Partridge Family.*

820. I feel like a criminal with a guest spot on *Charlie's Angels.*

821. I feel like the smart girl Andrea Zuckerman (Gabrielle Carteris) on *Beverly Hills 90210* who left the show in 1995.

822. I feel like Agent 99 (Barbara Feldon) on *Get Smart.*

823. I feel like a matron in drag (Eric Idle) in a *Monty Python* skit.

824. I feel like Cissy (Kathy Garver) on *Family Affair.*

825. I feel, depending on my mood, like either Patty or Cathy Lane (both played by Patty Duke) on *The Patty Duke Show.*

826. I feel like playing Fanny Dooley, a game I still remember from *Zoom.*

827. I feel like saying, "Fanny Dooley loves apples, but she hates fruit. Fanny Dooley loves poodles, but she hates dogs. Fanny Dooley loves chess, but she hates board games . . ." until you scream, "Stop!"

828. I feel like making you try to guess: why does Fanny love apples and poodles and chess?

829. I feel like you may have already figured out that Fanny only loves things with double letters.

830. I feel nostalgic.

831. I feel ripped off because I never got to be one of the rotating child hosts of *Zoom*—the show was shot in Boston and would have been an easy commute for me from Woonsocket, RI. And who knows, maybe I would have invested the money well and have become rich by now.

832. I feel ripped off because I always wanted to be in the audience of *Bozo's Big Top*, also filmed in Boston.

833. I feel jealous when my cousin gets tickets to *Bozo* somehow.

834. I feel jealous when I see his big head smile into the camera, his hand waving wildly to everyone in the TV audience.

835. I feel ripped off when we go to the new shopping plaza in Rhode Island where Bozo is making a guest appearance in a helicopter, but when he signs his picture, he doesn't even act like the real Bozo.

836. I feel disappointed, but try not to let my mother know.

837. I feel my mother's exhaustion, waiting out in the scorching parking lot of a new shopping plaza with her two kids who want, even more than to meet Bozo, to be on his TV show.

838. I feel like it must be really hard to raise kids.

839. I feel like you probably feel you should tell your children that's not the real Bozo, but then you also want them to have a good time and not be disappointed.

840. I feel like staying young and single forever, like Ann Marie (Marlo Thomas) on *That Girl*.

841. I feel that I should make my own kite with my own silhouette, just to get it out of my system.

842. I feel like taking my Denise-silhouette kite and flying it in Central Park.

843. I feel like Mary Ann (Dawn Wells) on *Gilligan's Island*.

844. I feel like someone who just won big bucks identifying the "Golden Melody" on *Name That Tune*.

845. I feel like Gloria Bunker (Sally Struthers) on *All in the Family*.

846. I feel I am much more liberal than my parents, but our differences aren't out in the open like they are on *All in the Family.*

847. I feel perplexed when I hear someone now use the word "meathead" or "dingbat."

848. I feel like I have to stop to remember what show made those phrases popular.

849. I feel like Sally Struthers, putting on weight and making pleas to fight hunger in third world children.

850. I feel good about my foster child in Colombia until my husband tells me it's a scam.

851. I feel like Sally Struthers being parodied on *South Park,* another current show I just remembered I like.

852. I feel like Aunt Bee Taylor (Frances Bavier) on *The Andy Griffith Show.*

853. I feel like Ralph Monroe (the girl carpenter played by Mary Grace Canfield) on *Green Acres.*

854. I feel like Elly May (Donna Douglas) on *The Beverly Hillbillies.*

855. I feel like wearing a rope for a belt like Elly May did.

856. I feel like acting really dumb.

857. I feel like Lou Ann Poovie (Gomer's girlfriend played by Elizabeth MacRae) on *Gomer Pyle, U.S.M.C.*

858. I feel like Rhoda Morgenstern (Valerie Harper) on *The Mary Tyler Moore Show.*

859. I feel like Laura Petrie (Mary Tyler Moore) on *The Dick Van Dyke Show.*

860. I feel like Victoria Winters (Alexandra Moltke) on *Dark Shadows.*

861. I feel frustrated when *Dark Shadows* is preempted by Watergate coverage.

862. I feel bored by most of the testimony.

863. I feel really upset when Nixon is impeached.

864. I feel—maybe because I'm a teenager—that I'll never vote, that everyone is a crook.

865. I feel like a crook sometimes.

866. I feel like I can relate to Democrats more than I can to Republicans.

867. I feel, though, that basically it's hard to relate to politicians at all.

868. I feel that politicians don't have the glamour of TV personalities, even though they are, in essence, TV personalities.

869. I feel that politicians could be more distinguishable from one another if they dressed differently.

870. I feel that I would vote for a woman in sari.

871. I feel that I would vote for a man in a Hawaiian shirt.

872. I feel that I would vote for anyone in an aqua bathing cap.

873. I feel that politicians sound fake when they try to be too earnest.

874. I feel like I should read the paper more closely than I do.

875. I feel like becoming a well-informed citizen.

876. I feel doomed when I'm too well informed.

877. I feel that escapism has probably saved my life.

878. I feel that escapism has probably saved a lot of people's lives.

879. I feel that escapism has probably ruined lives too.

880. I feel like Batman.

881. I feel like Robin.

882. I feel like Catwoman.

883. I feel like Alfred Pennyworth, the butler of the Batcave.

884. I feel like Archie, a regular redheaded guy.

885. I feel like Veronica, a snob.

886. I feel like Jughead.

887. I feel like Moose.

888. I feel like Reggie.

889. I feel like a benevolent crossing guard, waving all the TV characters of my childhood safely across the street.

890. I feel like Wilma, the first TV character to share a bed with her husband.

891. I feel like Betty.

892. I feel like Barney.

893. I feel like Fred, the first TV character to share a bed with his wife.

894. I feel that maybe I'm finally getting old, against my will.

895. I feel my gray hairs, which are coarser than the others.

896. I feel, as a feminist, conflicted about dyeing them, but of course I do anyway.

897. I feel that I should at the very least tell you that I have more than a few gray hairs, most prominently located at the temple region.

898. I feel that when I get enough gray hair, I'll stop dyeing it.

899. I feel that I'm in that awkward stage—with only gray hairs at the frame of my face.

900. I feel gray hair can actually be pretty glamorous. It's sort of like extremely blond hair, when you think of it.

Möbius Strip: Love Sex Food Death

            Nick
said, "Don't worry, I won't
ever die on you, OK?"
and for a second I
believed him.   My
cinnamon angel, his soft
eyebrows folding in
sleep.   My thighs
sticking together, a white
icing between.   A
village near Kashmir
called Hunza is supposedly
the closest thing on earth
to the fountain of youth—
no one born there gets a
cavity or heart attack.
People, on average, live
to one hundred.   The
stems of sunflowers, like
pogo sticks, rising out of
the ground.   I
wanted Nick to have that
power, to make a pact
with the universe to die
second, to be a gentleman
about death.   Hunza
is on a high mountain, the
sea level perfect for breathing
and hard for Hunza enemies
to get to.   His scalp

smells sweet, a mixture of
cave and sea foam.   Water
was still running from the
faucet when Will found Pearl,
hip to bathroom tile, a
shattered glass at her breast.
Though she was dead, he
sniffed lilac soap in the air.
Her lips were sticky with
newly applied maroon
lipstick.   We ate red
bean buns on Canal Street,
fire-hydrant waters spraying
the children and glistening
gray fish that stunk up
entire blocks.   "Pearl
never smelled dead," Will
kept saying.   Once
in Chinatown I ordered
sea cucumber (*not*
a vegetable) by mistake—
chunks of fatty sea slugs I
couldn't contemplate
swallowing.   Today
Nick ordered Pho-Beef.   I
said I wished he'd ordered
Po Beef so that I could
order Tinky Winky Shrimp
or La La with fried rice.
We both agreed on our love
of *The Teletubbies*—the
show that is like an acid

trip, everything in slow
motion, everything
done twice, that freaky
sun with a giggling baby
face.   Sometimes I
ovulate mansions and
magic.   Nick and I
were talking about this
the other day—what
we'd do if we ever went
blind.   Nick and I
don't usually agree on
food.   I thought
about teaching Nick
how to put on my lipstick,
now while I can still
see.   In Miami
we heard a radio
announcement for
cochinillo asado that
guaranteed the piglets sold
were younger than twenty-four
days which made me
really sad though Nick,
who's had *cochinillo*
asado, was saying *yum*
yum.   I'd just
read about the woman
whose surgeon sliced
off her entire eyelid
during a botched face
lift so now she can't

blink.   She softened
and crumbled, like a
cruller dipped in coffee
too long.   After
he came, his moon
belly glowing, his navel
grew dark as though I'd
just plucked a fruit stem
from it.   The bananas
were as ready as we
were, bright peaches
bristling, the green insides
and outs of kiwi and
lime.   You sudsed
the hollow under my
arm.   We both
confessed to the irrational
fear of having our hands
cut off.   Our first
apartment smelled of
curry, a yellow pollen
dusting the sink and
drawers.   My
favorite lunch ever was
grilled cheese and a teaberry
milkshake.   You
shampooed my hair
twice.   When I
worked in the supermarket,
there was a customer
without hands who could
lift ten pounds of potatoes

with a silver hook he'd
maneuver through the
bag's red mesh.   I was
always afraid the hook
would twist off.   I was
afraid to see his stub, afraid
I'd have to bend to the
floor to pick up that metal
question mark.

Beneficiary

A few years later, we found a bunch of old fingernail clippings inside his fancy clipper. The clipper was like a pencil sharpener that kept all the shavings inside a case so the person clipping wouldn't have to put a newspaper under his hands or feet. The nail bits curled like cheap yellow noodles, like bits of Ramen that fall to the bottom of the plastic package they come in. They smelled like a mixture of hospital death and belly-button lint. It seemed wrong to throw them in the trash, but I could tell you were embarrassed by them, so that's what we did, tossed them right next to the coffee grounds. But later I dug them out and burned them—I can't say why, there was something beating in my primitive gut. I picked them out and put them in the sink, then threw in a match, so no witch could use the clippings against him, I guess.

I felt the same way about the opened box of Cheerios, the razor, the bottle of Bayer Aspirin. I couldn't throw them away and I couldn't bring myself to pour a bowl of his leftover cereal and eat. My niece, only two, started to shake when we went to clean out the apartment. We didn't think she understood, but she did. She sat quietly in the corner and asked for her jacket because she was cold.

I bought three muffins for the Amtrak trip from New York to Rhode Island where he lived. No one needs three muffins in four hours, I know, unless one's inconsolable. I kept waiting for certain passengers to get off the train so I could eat the next muffin— blueberry, pumpkin, and corn. I wanted each passenger who got on to think that the second and third muffins were my first. My stomach began to clang and snarl. It was easier to obsess about what was in my Zaro's bag than to cry in public. I unbuttoned the top button of my jeans. I would need a very big black dress.

I almost got to be a pallbearer since many of the men in my family have bad backs. But one uncle was set against it, and I thought I should leave well enough alone. Funerals are a bad time for fighting.

Right after his death, I filled out an organ donation card. I wanted, as a dead woman, to give my cravings to someone else, to make a woman's straight hair curl. I wanted her to replicate the dreams I held in my heart, my liver, my eyes, whatever the doctors could use to save her. I wanted the live woman to dream one more of my dreams, or let my dreams collage with hers, our union a benevolent Frankenstein.

I used his VCR with alarming detachment, though sometimes at night I was afraid of the blinking lights. I wore his sweater, and then I got married. Later my husband wore his sweater.

I didn't want him to end, not his last shrinking bar of soap. I didn't want it to become gradually smaller then one day float down the drain. I couldn't throw away the shampoo or Aqua Velva. I puzzled at the rubber flowers he'd put in his tub so he wouldn't slip. I tried to peel one off before my sister gave his key back to the landlord. I wished I had recorded his voice.

I went to therapy where I cried for an hour straight. I caught the therapist starting to drift off, so I forced a wail to wake her up, to be my witness. The sleeping looked too much like the dead.

The old boyfriend called, the obligatory call, and that only made it worse. His having left, another kind of death. Soon after we talked, I dreamt that I died and that the doctors gave my old boyfriend my spleen. I was watching the operation from the ceiling, but in the middle of the procedure he woke up and said, "Wait a minute, I don't need a spleen to live." He walked out of the hospital, and the doctors threw my spleen into the trash.

Then I found out you could also donate your skeleton so I made arrangements to do that. Anything to help me live on, I guess. Anything to be useful. I was sure I hadn't done enough in this life. And sure I never would.

I sometimes fantasize about the skeleton I'll be—jangling on wheels on my way to anatomy class, dance class, figure-drawing class. Some of the students, I imagine, will be spooked out, but most will look at me and sober up. Maybe I'll be the source of mini-epiphanies at last.

But then someday even the beneficiary of my transplant will be gone. The school where I donated my skeleton will no longer exist—the building, the teachers, the students. My skeleton will be gone and the dust my skeleton makes, and all the human dancers and all the animal dancers will be gone. The paintings will be gone, and all the minerals that made such luscious pigments. Science will no longer exist—the goggles, the petri dishes, the computers, all dead. Trees will be gone and paper and ink and books. The films will be gone, the music, and the math. I will be gone, but I will miss you if I'm still able to miss anything, that is, if some particle of me remains and some particle of you.

And I tell my husband: if I die first, I'll try to come back and tell you what it's like. I'll try to translate death into English or at least kiss the back of your neck while you sleep. It is the real promise of all true lovers, the promise that has never been kept. And then all the great earth itself will be gone, and maybe even our moon and stars, all the other planets. All our fingernails.

But that will not be the end of it.

It's true. The earth is no longer there, but something there are no words for yet, something like a tiny blue swivel chair, will be spinning wildly in its place.

Carbó Frescos

Duhamel (1961–2061) was born in Providence, Rhode Island, USA. A pupil of Lux, Valentine, and Burkard, her poems had a sense of volume that was indicative of the postmodern literature of her era. She was one of the first to produce frescos made entirely of words. While several critics of her time found her work "chatty" and "easily forgotten," Duhamel herself had hoped her poetry was of "an intensely human significance." Her most famous fresco cycle (written directly on the wall of a handball court in a place once known as the Hollywood Broadwalk, Florida) is one depicting the life of her husband Nick Carbó (1964–2066). Carbó was born in the Philippines and Duhamel, it is said, often romanticized his life story. After years of unsuccessfully pestering him to write a memoir, she decided to write his memoir, fresco-style, for him. For many years, historians debated whether or not "Carbó Frescos" were indeed the work of Carbó himself. Helen Bloom Vendler (3582–3641, a historian who could trace her lineage back to Helen Vendler and Harold Bloom, two famous literary critics of Duhamel's time [who, ironically, ignored Duhamel completely]) is credited with finding actual writing samples of Duhamel so that the frescos could at last be truly attributed to her. "Carbó Frescos" miraculously survived coastal erosion, wars, and plagues and are now on permanent display in the "Carbó Fresco Room" in the New Mexico Museum of Art and History.

The story of Nick Carbó begins on the south wall:

1. Nick Carbó is born a peasant to Filipino farm workers. He is characterized by Duhamel as a "brown angel in a manger." Some analysts have said that Duhamel put her husband up on a pedestal, as a Christ figure, but others suggest that the word "manger" is used in a secular way or perhaps even satirically.

2. When he is ten days old, Nick Carbó is adopted by a Spanish family and taken to live in a mansion with dozens of pet dogs and tennis courts. His favorite maid, Rosita, often carries him off to bed. Carbó's sense of smell is fine-tuned, Duhamel writes, "by the musk scent of Rosita's scalp." Duhamel describes in detail Carbó's childhood bedroom, his sombrero, and his wagon. So fully real-

ized is Carbó's early childhood many speculate that Duhamel interviewed Carbó extensively and or worked from photographs given to her by Carbó's parents.

3. Nick Carbó is left alone in a pool. In this rather terrifying fresco, Duhamel recounts a three-year-old Carbó taken for a swimming lesson and forgotten there by his parents who are at a party. One by one, the young swimming students are picked up, and eventually even the swimming teacher leaves. Frigid and terrified, Carbó keeps afloat in his black-and-white swimming trunks. He can't find his towel. He can't see his flip-flops. When his parents finally arrive to pick him up, they are tipsy, unaware of the anxiety tiny Carbó has suffered. Duhamel reproduces this nightmare of near-drowning with zeal and authenticity as she also nearly drowned in a pool at a young age. (See her early sonnet "Nearly Drowning at Six.")

4. Nick Carbó has a crush on a grade-school girl who looks surprisingly like Duhamel as a young girl. Though Carbó won't meet Duhamel until he is in his late twenties, Duhamel portrays this crush's sole purpose as readying Carbó to meet Duhamel later. In this innocent and carefree fresco, Duhamel all but imagines herself as the young American in the International School in the Philippines. Much significance is put on this particular fresco, as Duhamel includes none of Carbó's later love interests. Duhamel has essentially erased all other women in Carbó's life but herself.

The story of Nick Carbó continues on the west wall:

5. Nick Carbó visits New York City as a teenager. He buys a hot dog from a street vendor. He and his family go to see the Broadway play *A Chorus Line*. His mother's wallet is stolen in the hotel lobby. His father yells at a clerk in Bloomingdale's when she won't accept his traveler's checks. Carbó is served cold cereal for breakfast, and never having had it in the Philippines, eats it dry not knowing he should pour milk on it. Young Carbó looks at America with simultaneous disdain and admiration. This theme will be picked up again and again in Carbó's own poetry. (See especially his early book *Secret Asian Man*.) Duhamel's implicit

fear in this fresco is that Carbó also transfers the contempt he feels for the United States onto Duhamel.

6. Nick Carbó joins the demonstrations against Marcos, a corrupt president who ruled at that time in the Philippines, and is sprayed by tear gas. Duhamel is especially taken with Carbó's youthful political zeal. Though Carbó is of the upper class, he identifies with the plight of the people. Duhamel describes Carbó's tears as "the tears of all the Philippines" and she imagines families ruined by prostitution, disease, and malnutrition, and children picking through mounds of trash. She tries to create an alternate reality for Carbó, one that speculates what his life would have been like had he not been adopted. She hypothesizes that he cuts off his own arm so that he's a more effective beggar.

7. Nick Carbó plays tennis at Manila Bay's Army and Navy Country Club, to which his family belongs. Duhamel spends dozens of lines describing Carbó's arm and his serve, hearkening back to the imagined amputated arm of the previous fresco. In this, Duhamel's most surreal fresco, the tennis balls Carbó hits become women's high-heeled shoes. Imelda Marcos, the wife of the then Filipino president, was known to have been an avid shoe collector. Her shoes became a symbol of the administration's decadence and waste. Originally Duhamel wanted to write her poem fresco on the ground of a clay tennis court, but could not get permission from the Mayor of Hollywood, FL, and settled for the walls of a handball court.

The story of Nick Carbó continues on the north wall:

8. Nick Carbó comes to Bennington College in Vermont to study. In this fresco, Carbó tastes snowflakes, makes a snowman, and uses a piece of cardboard as a sled. Though he is a young man, Duhamel illustrates Carbó with the exuberance of a child. The falling snow is like a pleasing death, a death to Carbó's life in the Philippines, as he will never return there to live full time. The falling snow covers him as though bathing him in a new optimistic innocence. The swirling snow blinds Carbó and freezes him in time. Here in Vermont, he will learn to write and work backwards to uncover his complicated boyhood.

9. Nick Carbó falls in love with Denise Duhamel. This is the largest and most detailed of the Carbó frescos, owing perhaps to the exaggerated role Duhamel felt she had in shaping the life of Carbó. The fresco begins with the first night the two make love. Carbó accidentally swallows a strand of Duhamel's hair, and Duhamel runs with this image—the way her very fiber is inside him, the way her very essence will always be part of Carbó's creation from here on in. The fresco embellishes dualities: Carbó's east and Duhamel's west; Carbó's privilege and Duhamel's working-class background; Carbó's yang and Duhamel's yin; Carbó's yin and Duhamel's yang. Carbó will go on to live many more years, losing and regaining his fortune (see Tometra Finkelstein's biography *Secret Carbó: Dialectic of the Asian Avant-Garde*). Yet Duhamel ends the narrative of her frescos here, with roses adorning their bed as Carbó and Duhamel sleep holding hands, dreaming, one would guess, the same dream.

"Noah and Joan" is for for Marcia Adams.

"Möbius Strip: Forgetfulness" is after Luc Etienne and is a variation of his Möbius strip poems. For the complete Möbius strip effect, xerox two copies of the poem and trim away the title and any extra paper on either side of the poem and under the last line of the poem, which now reads "little dog." Scotch tape, glue, or staple the strips of paper in a long row, so that both copies run parallel to each other, but in a mirrored image. The first lines of both copies, "   she tries," should be back to back to one another, and so on. Loop the poem into a cylinder, then twist it once before splicing and scotch taping what is currently the first line and last line together. In the 3-D version, the last line/first line should read, "little dog   she tries".

"Our Americano" was inspired by the *Dictionary of American Slang,* compiled and edited by Harold Wentworth and Stuart Berg Flexner, published by Thomas Y. Crowell Company, 1960.

"Pituitary Theft" is composed of English subtitles used in films made in Hong Kong.

"Love Which Took Its Symmetry for Granted" is a collage made up of e-mails I received September 11 to September 18, 2001, from Sherry Busbee, Bill Cohen, Laetitia Duhamel, Maria Graham, Kathleen Rockwell Lawrence, Amy Lemmon, Sharon Olinka, Michael Sherman, Eileen Tabios, Susan Wheeler, and Susan Yuzna. I also used forwarded announcements from Florida International University, the *Chronicle of Higher Education,* Poets House, and American Airlines. Article quotes (from Gary Kamiya, Mary Ann Weaver, Robert Fisk, and Bob Wing) were also forwarded to me via e-mail. The quote from Derek Walcott comes from his Nobel Lecture. Walter Benjamin's quote is from "Theses on the Philosophy of History."

"Möbius Strip: Love Sex Food Death" is also after Luc Etienne and is a variation of his Möbius strip poems. For the complete "Möbius Strip" effect, follow the directions for "Möbius Strip: Forgetfulness." In the 3-D version of "Möbius Strip: Love Sex Food Death," the last line/first line should read, "question mark.   Nick".

"Lawless Pantoum" was written after an e-mail forward about the supposed laws governing sexual conduct in Lebanon; Bahrain; Indonesia; Guam; Hong Kong; Columbia; Bolivia; Liverpool, England; and Maryland, USA.

"Beneficiary" is for Wilfred Bourgeois, in memory.

Grateful acknowledgment is made to the editors and staff members of the magazines in which work from *Two and Two*, sometimes in slightly different form, first appeared: *Artful Dodge* ("Möbius Strip: Love Sex Food Death"); *Barrow Street* ("Incest Taboo"); *Black Warrior Review* ("Beneficiary," under the title "Epilogue"); *Bryant Literary Review* ("Our Americano"); *Chelsea* ("The Problem with Woody Allen"); *Chiron Review* ("Crater Face"); *Crazyhorse* ("Möbius Strip: Forgetfulness"); *5 AM* ("Napping on the Afternoon of My Thirty-ninth Birthday," "Dream Interpretations," and "Carbó Frescos"); *Mid-American Review* ("The Accident"); *Mississippi Review* ("Embarazar"); *Montserrat Review* ("Noah and Joan"); *Poet Lore* ("Egg Rolls"); *Prairie Schooner* ("*Mille et un sentiments*," lines 1–100); *Quarterly West* ("Warning"); *Sentence: A Journal of Prose Poetics* ("*Mille et un sentiments*," lines 401–500); *TriQuarterly* ("*Mille et un sentiments*," lines 801–900); *Wake Up Heavy* ("Pituitary Theft"); *West Branch* ("Lawless Pantoum"); and *x-Stream* ("Love Which Took Its Symmetry for Granted").

Lines 1–100; 401–500; and 801–900 of "Mille et un sentiments" were reprinted in a limited-edition book, *Mille et un sentiments* (2005). "Noah and Joan" was reprinted in *Wild and Whirling Words: A Poetic Conversation* (2004). "Crater Face" was reprinted in the online magazine *Cortland Review* and in the anthologies *Bum Rush the Page: A Def Poetry Jam* (2001) and *Like Thunder: Poets Respond to Violence in America* (2002). "Incest Taboo" was reprinted in *The Best American Poetry 2000*. "Napping on the Afternoon of My Thirty-ninth Birthday" was reprinted in *Great American Prose Poems: From Poe to the Present* (2003). Thanks to the anthology editors: H. L. Hix, Tony Medina, Virgil Suarez, Ryan Van Cleave, David Lehman, and Rita Dove.

Gratitude to Yaddo, the MacDowell Colony, Fundación Valparaíso, and Civitella Ranieri for tremendous hospitality.

Thanks to my parents for permitting me to tell their story, to Eamon Grennan and Kira Grennan for their Archie knowledge, and to Angela Ball for giving me the real lowdown on Frank Perdue and RU486.

And a special *merci* to those who helped in shaping this manuscript: Tom Fink, Ed Ochester, Elizabeth Powell, Maureen Seaton, and especially Nick Carbó and Stephanie Strickland.